REFLECTIONS

Ricardo Montalban
with Bob Thomas

REFLECTIONS
A Life in Two Worlds

1980
DOUBLEDAY & COMPANY, INC.
GARDEN CITY, NEW YORK

Excerpt from *Man and Superman* by
Bernard Shaw. Reprinted by permission
of The Society of Authors.

ISBN: 0-385-12878-9
Library of Congress Catalog Card Number: 77-15166

REFLECTIONS

FRIDAY

The station wagon pointed down the hill and glided along Doheny Drive to Sunset Boulevard. As I had feared, the Friday afternoon traffic on Sunset was heavy, and I cut down Holloway Drive to Santa Monica Boulevard, where it was worse. I tried another route, Fountain Avenue; it was crowded, but at least the cars kept moving.

I had expected the freeways to be jammed on a summer Friday, with people heading for weekends or longer holidays in the mountains and at the beaches. Surprisingly, traffic on the Hollywood Freeway was traveling swiftly, and except for some stop-and-go after the interchange, progress was easy on the San Bernardino Freeway. I settled back in the seat and tuned in KGRB. The station plays only big-band music of the 1930s and 1940s, and the sounds of Glenn Miller and Tommy Dorsey put me in a fine, reminiscing mood.

How long since I had been on a retreat? Four years? Five? I wondered at how the time had vanished. They had been busy years, scrambling from television roles to stage plays in order to keep my career alive; then, with the television series, finding my life so busy that I scarcely had time to think. These have been years of personal change, too, as Georgiana and I adjusted to a new life together, without children.

We had looked forward to our vacation at the end of the first season of "Fantasy Island." The series had been a joyful experience for me, but also a time-consuming one. I had spent more time with Hervé Villechaize than with my wife. Fortunately, I am very fond of Hervé, so it has not been a burden to be with him.

Georgie and I would have a month together, and we enjoyed considering where we might vacation. The Greek islands were enticing, or St. Peters Island. But what about Yucatán? I had never been to that fabulous part of the land of my birth. Yes, we agreed we would go to Yucatán for two restful weeks of sunning and swimming and seeing the Mayan ruins.

It was a glorious time, even though Georgie acquired a persistent cough which eventually transferred to me. The friendly Yucatán sun and the cobalt-blue water made the concerns of our day-to-day living seem far away. They were soon to overtake us.

At the end of the second week, my agent telephoned. Chrysler wanted me to film a thirty-second commercial. I would have to go back to California immediately. That meant canceling the third week of the vacation, when we had planned to visit my brother Pedro in Mexico City.

The commercial was filmed in Monterey, California, and I was pleased with its humorous quality, something different from others I had done. I returned home and found the first script of the new season of "Fantasy Island." That evening Georgiana fixed me a drink, and I sat down in a comfortable chair to read. After I had read ten or twelve pages, the telephone rang. Georgiana answered it.

Her face was white when she came into the room.

"Brace yourself, sweetheart, brace yourself," she said. "Pedro is dead."

I was overwhelmed by sorrow and regret. Pedro was my second-oldest brother, and I had known his warm presence from my earliest memories. It was inconceivable that he was gone. How sorry I was that my schedule for that week had been changed. If only . . .

I had to reach Mexico City as soon as possible. I called the airlines and discovered the only flight that night was one leaving at twelve-thirty, a "red-eye special." The passengers were jammed like cattle, and Georgiana and I lay awake the entire journey, trying to reconcile ourselves to the loss of Pedro. It was impossible.

The plane arrived in Mexico City at dawn, and Georgiana and I went directly to the home of my old friends Maximiliano and Cecilia Escheverria. I learned my sister, Carmen, had arrived from Torreón, and I reached her by telephone. We consoled each other, and I said I would take a shower and try to close my eyes for half an hour, then I would go to the mortuary.

When I arrived, Pedro's body was not there! It had been removed for an autopsy which the law required when someone died in a public place; Pedro had been lunching with a friend in a restaurant when his heart failed. The coroner determined that Pedro had died of natural causes, and the body was returned. I signed for it and began making the necessary arrangements.

His daughter told me that Pedro apparently had some premonition of his death. He had said to her, "When I die, I want two things. First, no tears at my funeral; I want my friends and relatives to have a drink or two, and I want a mariachi band to play. Second, since I was born in Spain, I want to be buried with the Spanish flag."

"I can't promise you there will be no tears," his daughter replied. "I'm not going to have people get drunk at your funeral, and certainly there will be no mariachi music. But this I will assure you, Father: you will be buried with the Spanish flag."

And there it was, on his chest in the coffin. His children had asked me to look at Pedro in death, and I did so with some reluctance. They had told me that he had died with his face in the contortion of pain, but the undertaker's art had given him a pleasant expression by forcing the corners of the mouth upward into the charade of a smile.

As I held the lid of the coffin open, I looked down at Pedro in his best suit, the Spanish flag, and a poem by one of his grandchildren on his chest, and I started to sob. Uncontrollably I shook with sorrow, and as I did, I jostled the coffin. His head moved from side to side, and Pedro seemed to be admonishing me: "For heaven's sake, Ricardo, don't take it so seriously; it's just another chapter in the human comedy."

The cortege followed the mournful course through the Mexico City streets to the Spanish cemetery, a verdant place of great comfort to the living, though the dead could not care less. The cemetery was crowded, and we had had trouble finding a plot for Pedro; we finally bought two plots. They were far removed from the parking area, and the mourners— Pedro had many friends—walked behind the six uniformed men who wheeled the coffin through the tree-shaded paths.

I held my sister tightly in my arms as the coffin was lowered into the earth. Both of us were overcome by sorrow, but we had to stand there and witness, according to Mexican law, the sealing of the grave. A worker climbed into the grave and placed three cement slabs on the coffin. Then he clambered out and dropped in wet cement to conclude the job.

Friends approached to offer their condolences to Carmen and me and Pedro's children. In the midst of this, the chief of the funeral attendants came to me and said the men had concluded their work and now they expected to be tipped. With tears still streaming down my face, I gave him a handful of bills. Then the cement man came to me and announced, "You have been served." I handed him whatever money I had left. I wanted nothing more than to be gone from that place.

As the family started to leave the graveside, the heavens opened up. First sheets of rain and then stinging pellets of hail hurled down, chilling us to the bone. The sky had been blue twenty minutes before; now we were caught in a torrential downpour. We skidded over the mud and finally reached our cars, soggy and disheveled. How Pedro must have laughed; even then he seemed to be playing a joke on us.

My brother Carlos telephoned. He had just returned to New York from a European tour and had received the sorrowful news. "I must come right away," he said.

"No, don't, Carlos," I told him. "It is all over now. There is nothing you can do."

Pedro's face was in my mind throughout the flight back to Los Angeles. He looked just like Don Quixote, with this difference: his was a happy countenance, not a sad one. Everyone loved him. He visited me twice in Los Angeles and once in New York, and all my friends were immediately drawn to him. All his life he had been like that; he was everyone's favorite member of the family.

When had I last seen him in life? I think it was in Cuernavaca two or three years ago, when I was working in an episode of "Columbo." He was smiling as always, but he didn't seem well. Pedro had contracted malaria while working in the isthmus of Tehuantepec, and his health was never as good after that. In his later years he suffered from pancreatitis. Doctors told him that he absolutely could not drink, but of course he didn't mind them. He enjoyed the company of friends too much. Besides, he worked for Pedro Domecq as a public relations man, and he felt it was his duty to share a glass of sherry or two with his clients. If Pedro had any failing, it was perhaps that he sometimes drank too much. Not that he had a drinking problem, not at all. He simply wanted everyone to have a good time.

There was an air of sadness about him when we met last in Cuernavaca, and I believe it was because he had separated from his wife. He still loved her very much, and he may have been lonely in his final years. All the more reason I wish I had seen my beloved Pedro more often.

Fortunately, I plunged into work as soon as I returned to Los Angeles. Chrysler asked me to fly to Detroit to take part in the presentation of the new car models to fleet buyers. On my return, I immediately began the second season of "Fantasy Island."

The weekdays were filled with long hours of work in the studio and at the arboretum, where the exterior scenes are filmed. But on the weekend Pedro again filled my heart and mind. It had been a milestone in my life—the passing of the first member of the family in my generation. Such a loss hits hard, and I found myself beset with questions.

Who am I at this point in my life?

Am I too caught up in the pettiness of day-to-day living, so that I have lost sight of the goals I once set for myself?

Where am I going?

Do I see only the brushstrokes of my life, instead of standing back and studying the whole painting?

I needed time and a place to assess my life, past, present, and future. That is why I was driving eastward on the San Bernardino Freeway amid the strains of "The Chattanooga Choo-Choo."

The directions to Manresa Retreat House were clear: take the San Bernardino to Freeway 605, off on the Foothill Freeway to the Citrus Avenue exit in Azusa; north on Citrus to Foothill Boulevard and Palm Drive.

I headed up the gentle slope, passing between rows of towering palm trees. They had not been so tall when I came there thirty-one years before. That was when I made my first retreat in California. I had made two visits to Manresa in those early years, then I had gone to other retreats, mostly Benedictine. Now I was back with the Jesuits.

The setting was ideal. Manresa is surrounded by a wholesale nursery, certainly one of the largest in the world. The rows of potted shrubs and trees, all clustered according to species, stretch for miles—enough plants to landscape a national park. They create a variegated green carpet, a restful surrounding for Manresa.

As I drove into the courtyard, I saw that the Retreat House was changed from when I had seen it last.

Before, the dining room and the chapel were contained in the imposing Norman château. A new wing on the west side now contained the dining room and kitchen, and the chapel occupied a separate building to the east. I was greeted inside the front door by Father Von der Ahe, who registered me and gave me directions to my room for the weekend. It was down the hill in a new building, with rooms more sparingly furnished but just as comfortable as a Holiday Inn.

After unpacking, I had time before dinner to study the instructions that Father Von der Ahe had given me. The schedule for Friday:

7:00 Dinner and Welcome
8:30 Conference in Chapel
9:00 Celebration of Liturgy
9:30 Evening Prayers

The first item on the instruction folder concerned Silence: "The fine regard for silence is one of the most treasured traditions of a Manresa retreat. Silence in a retreat is not only GOLDEN, it is PRICELESS! Strict silence is demanded during the entire retreat. You cannot make a good retreat unless you are recollected —and you cannot be recollected unless you keep silence. You also owe your fellow retreatants the courtesy of Silence, because the silence of man makes audible the voice of God!"

Ah yes, silence. That is the part of a retreat that always disturbs me beforehand. How can I possibly remain silent for virtually all of forty-two hours? After all, I work at an extremely vocal profession, in which the ability to communicate is vitally important.

Yet, as I learn during every retreat, there are other ways to communicate than with words. Often a man's movements, his physical attitudes can prove more eloquent than anything he can utter with his mouth.

Too often words get in the way; they don't really express what we mean. I have found that at the end of every retreat I cherish the silence. It refreshes the soul after life in a noisy world.

The steeple bell clanged the call to dinner, and if anyone mistook the summons, a persistent buzzer added emphasis. These sounds would become familiar through the weekend, and I regarded them not as a schoolboy dreading his next class, but as notice of a new adventure.

Father Von der Ahe led the blessing before dinner, and together we recited the prayer of St. Ignatius for generosity:

"Dearest Lord, teach me to be generous,
teach me to serve Thee as Thou deservest;
to give and not to count the cost;
to fight and not to heed the wounds;
to toil and not to seek for rest;
to labor and not ask for reward,
save that of knowing that I am doing Thy will."

Then we sat down to a robust dinner of lettuce salad, baked ham, creamed potatoes, green beans, fudge ripple ice cream and—miracle of miracles—a bottle of *French* cabernet sauvignon, 1971.

Dinner offered the first opportunity to view the other retreatants and to become acquainted—our silence had not yet been imposed—with the three persons with whom I would be having my meals until Sunday. There were forty of us in the dining room at tables of four and six, and I couldn't imagine a more varied cross section of American life. Ages ranged from fifteen to the seventies. There were crew cuts, longhairs, and baldies. Several seemed to have known a lifetime of hard physical labor. One fellow looked like a Hollywood wheeler-dealer, another like a schoolteacher. As I learned from reading the list of retreatants, one was a doctor, another a local judge. A man brought three of his teen-age sons, another came with his grown-up son. There were a couple beside myself of Mexican heritage, a black man, and one or more Protestants. Non-Catholics are welcome and are invited to attend all the exercises except Confession and Holy Communion.

The retreatant who most captured my attention was David, who sat opposite me at the dinner table. I had noticed that he walked with great difficulty, swinging forward a leg that was shorter than the other. He was in his early twenties, a nice-looking young man with a well-trimmed mustache and thick brown hair. At first glance, he might have appeared a rising young stockbroker. But when he started to eat, he was excruciating to watch. He grasped his knife and fork with great difficulty, and it was minutes before he could cut the ham and lift it to his mouth. Pouring a glass of water from the pitcher was a major project, and he spilled some onto the table. He tried to join in the dinner conversation, but his words came falteringly. Yet through it all he remained cheerful. He struggled to open an envelope of Sanka as the young waitress stood beside him with a pot of hot water. After he finally accomplished the feat, he gazed up and told her with a smile, "Patience is virtue."

After dinner Father Von der Ahe explained the schedule and urged us all to promptness. Smoking was allowed, "but a retreat is a time to restrict and restrain yourself." The telephone could be used, "but the spirit of the retreat silence demands that only necessary calls be made."

"Silence will begin after chapel this evening," Father Von der Ahe remarked. "That's a curious way to

greet you, by asking you to remain silent. But we feel
that you should spend your time here listening, not
talking. When you are alone with yourself, who
knows when and how God will talk to you?"

There was time after dinner for sociability, and several of the other retreatants remarked to me about the
Cordoba commercials and "Fantasy Island." I was
pleased to hear one of the men say, "That's one show
that I can let my children watch without any concern
that they will see something objectionable."

I asked Father Von der Ahe if he came from the
prominent Los Angeles family that bears the same
name. Indeed he did, and he told a story: "I was a
convert, and none of the rest of my family could understand it, especially my father. I remember when I
was in seminary, he came up to see me in a beautiful
Packard touring car—this was 1929. After we had
talked for a while, he held out the keys to the Packard
—and his house. 'These are yours if you will leave
with me,' he said. 'No, Father, I can't,' I said, and he
was very disappointed. But he came to my ordination
—my other relatives didn't—and later in life he became a Catholic."

The chapel was a cool and comforting refuge. The
walls were white-painted brick, the oak-beam ceiling a
rich brown. A bronze of the crucified Christ hung
over the altar. We retreatants sat on comfortable
chairs instead of hard benches.

Father O'Gara introduced himself. He would be
our retreat master for the weekend, the one who
would preside at the regular chapel conferences, who
would lead us in our spiritual search, and would hear
our confessions. He was a strong, vital presence, a
man in his fifties, I would guess, an Irishman with an
almost combative approach to his mission of conducting us to God's presence.

"This will be an *encounter* with God," he told us.
"You know of marriage encounters and other kinds of
encounters; this one is different. You will need to shut
out everything else. Forget about your everyday concerns; they are unimportant now. This is not a time
for conversing with your friends. This is a time to converse with God."

Father O'Gara related the story of the stonecutters.
A priest walked by as the three men were laboring,
and he asked each of them what he was doing.

"I'm making money—eighteen dollars a day," said
the first man.

"I'm cutting stone, making little ones out of big
ones," said the second.

The third man replied, "Father, we're building a
church."

Father O'Gara commented, "That man was not
only a poet but a realist. You men are also in the con-
struction business. You're here to put your house in
order. You start with the foundation, and then you
put up the walls and roof, and finally you decorate the
interior. The foundation is this: Do you believe in
God?"

After Mass and Holy Communion, we had our evening prayers. All forty of us were silent as we emerged
into the soft summer night. I could hear the faraway
noise of a rock band playing at a Friday night party. A
freight train rumbled in the distance. There was little
other sound except crickets and the palm fronds that
rustled in the warm summer breeze. It was a time for
reminiscence.

It was a story I had heard many times and never tired of.
The time was early in this century, the place was Soria, a town
of New Castile, known chiefly for the twelfth-century churches

of San Nicholas and Santo Domingo and the fine old Romanesque cloisters of the Convent of San Juan.

Jenaro was a handsome young man, energetic and ambitious. After his mother died, his father married a woman who made the boy's life miserable. Jenaro left his father's house in Valladolid when he was thirteen and found work in Soria as apprentice in a dry goods store, where he proved himself to be a good worker.

Every day Jenaro rode his bicycle from his rooming house to the dry goods store, returning for the lunch hour. He was pedaling home one afternoon when he glanced up at the balcony of a house and saw a girl of rare beauty. She sat in the window fanning herself, oblivious of his presence, and she seemed the most beautiful girl he had ever seen. He made certain to follow the same route returning to the store. Again she failed to notice him.

He rode his bicycle along the street every day, and finally she saw him riding by. She watched him the following day, and he nodded to her. To his total delight, she nodded back. Now the highlight of each day came when he glided past her house on the bicycle and she smiled her recognition from the balcony.

One day he was glancing up to her when his bicycle came to an abrupt halt. He saw to his horror that he had struck a plump woman bearing a basket of laundry on her head. As Jenaro fell to the ground he saw a blizzard of shirts, blouses, napkins, and handkerchiefs flying through the air. Then he felt his head being beaten with the basket, wielded by the furious washing woman, who added a stream of invective to the attack. The miserable Jenaro glanced up and saw the beautiful girl laughing behind her fan.

For a month the embarrassed young man avoided the street where the girl lived. But he had to return, and to his relief, her smiles seemed warmer. He felt emboldened to ask the girl's mother if he could pay her a call. The mother made inquiries about the young man and was told that he was indeed serious and hard-working. He was allowed to come to the house in the evening and meet the girl, whose name was Ricarda Merino. Properly chaperoned, of course.

And so the courtship began. By the standards of Spain during that time, the romance was passionate. That is to say that during the five minutes Jenaro and Ricarda were allowed to be alone, they expressed their devotion to each other. He was not the only suitor of the beautiful and intelligent young lady. But she esteemed him above all the others, and she expressed her preference to her father. He agreed with her choice, despite the young man's modest salary at the dry goods store.

"Ricarda my dear, this young man may never provide the luxuries of life," said her father, "but you will always have his respect and love."

So they were married. The local newspaper, *El Avisador Numantino*, reported the event in an edition of 1903:

> At 5 o'clock yesterday morning, Nuptial Mass was held in the Church of San Pedro in this capital to celebrate the indissoluble matrimonial vows of the beautiful señorita of Soria, Ricarda Merino, and the esteemed young man, Don Jenaro Montalban.
>
> The union was blessed by the Soria priest Don Pedro Merino, who is the brother of the bride.
>
> The new couple left after the ceremony on their honeymoon to Burgo de Osma and Valladolid. May they receive our heartfelt felicitations and best wishes for a blessed life together.

Another year, another balcony. It was 1956 in the northern Mexico city of Torreón. On a quiet tree-shaded street a mature, still lovely woman sat on the balcony of a two-story house. Her husband was on the walk below, white-haired and elegant in his Sunday-best black suit. He called up to her.

"Are you sure you will not go to the wedding, my dear?" he asked.

"No, Jenaro, I do not feel well enough, and I will only dampen the festivities."

"That you could never do. But if you cannot go, I will give an extra kiss to the bride, just for you."

"Of course, darling. And Jenaro—"

"Yes, Ricarda?"

"Only two or three dances. Do not try to show up the young people."

Her husband smiled. "I will try, my dear."

She watched him fondly as he strode vigorously down the street and disappeared around the corner. She never saw him alive again. My father toppled over on the street and died instantly of a brain clot.

They had fifty-three years together. Fifty-three years of happiness, sorrow, prosperity, bad times, joy, disappointment, but always—love. I have never known two people who were more in love.

When I first started in American movies, interviewers tried to hang the title of Latin lover on me. I even appeared opposite Lana Turner in a film called *Latin Lovers*. Actors from Rudolph Valentino to Marcello Mastroianni have been stuck with the sobriquet, and I've never been certain what it means. If being a Latin lover implies needing a new conquest every day, preferably two, then I find nothing admirable in such a man. Of course it is easy to be obsessed with the chase and to seek the thrill of change. But that doesn't take much imagination. Dogs do the same thing.

I consider my father the greatest of Latin lovers. I'm convinced of it. For fifty-three years he was always faithful, always respectful of my mother. He enjoyed an active sex life to the end of his days, and he was never bored. Imagine the romanticism that it took to keep a love affair going all those years! To my mind *that* is being a Latin lover.

The sense of harmony between my mother and father pervaded our home. Not that they were always peaceful. My mother was very sensitive, my father was high-strung, with a quick temper. Essentially he was a happy man, with a sunny, optimistic view of life despite the business setbacks he had in his lifetime. Mother was not exactly a pessimist, more of a realist; she was always ready to point out the practicality in Father's schemes.

Father was blond and blue-eyed, medium height, a strongly built man with strong hands. He liked to use them to work in carpentry, a hobby I inherited from him. He enjoyed puttering around his workshop on his day off from work, making little things. He respected his body and kept in trim physical condition. No excess in anything. Wine with the meal, yes. A good cigar on Sundays. He never overdid anything—except to dance. Parties in Torreón were filled with music of guitars and violins, and Father would leap out of his chair and start the dancing. He was smoothly expert in Castilian *jota*, which was done with elegance and style in his native Valladolid. Father also loved to lift his heels in the *chotis*, which is native to Madrid. He had his quieter moments. He was a great reader, and most of all he enjoyed dominoes. Every Sunday he walked to the club near our house and spent hours over domino games with his cronies. Mostly I remember him as a vigorous man. You never strolled with him; always he walked briskly, swinging his arms like a drill sergeant. The only time he walked slowly was when he escorted my mother. Then she put her arm in his, and they ambled down the street. I never saw them walking together when they weren't arm in arm.

Mother was sensitive but practical. She had been given an excellent education in Soria and could converse in Latin with the priests. She was widely read and an expert in Cervantean studies. No matter what the occasion, she could usually provide a proverb from *Don Quixote*. Such as, "A closed mouth catches no flies." Or, "Tell me thy company and I'll tell you what thou art." As you might expect, Mother was a fabulous cook, combining the best of Spanish and Mexican cuisines. I remember that when she called "Ready!" from the kitchen, I always ran to the table. Among her greatest dishes were *fabada*, an Asturian peasant delicacy made with large white beans, *jamón serrano*, a Spanish ham like prosciuto but drier and tastier, and blood sausages. Or *cocido*, a Castilian peasant dish made with garbanzo beans. And the bread—*bolillos!* How I loved coming home from school and smelling the aroma of freshly baked *bolillos*. I liked to take one of the rolls, scoop out the middle, and place inside a little bar of cooking chocolate. I munched on the roll as I did my homework.

Do you know that my mouth waters as I recollect Mexican dishes of my youth? Nothing else that is edible can make me do that.

My mother's house was immaculate. Even in times when the family fortunes were dwindling, we always had the cleanest linens, the most satisfying meals, including a first-class bottle of wine. My brothers, my sister, and I wore the finest clothes of any of the students in our schools, and we were always enrolled in the best possible schools. That was our parents' philosophy: in the necessities of life, nothing should be stinted. The luxuries? They were something else. I never had a bicycle, for example. My parents made me believe that a bicycle was a luxury the family could not afford. Only later did I realize the real reason: they were afraid for my safety on the busy Torreón streets.

Of course I yearned for a bike. But I understood and accepted my parents' rationale for not giving me one.

Religion was an irreplaceable adjunct to our family life. Mother said her Rosary every day, and she went to church every day if she was able. Father attended Mass every Sunday, as did the children. It was a very orderly, well-disciplined way of life for all of us.

Mother was more the disciplinarian, yet she had the wisdom to understand the man's role. Her voice saying "Don't do this, don't do that" all day carried no weight. She realized that the man's low tones of authority had more effect. So she waited for Father to return home and mete out the punishment. How I dreaded that! And yet the chastisement was always administered with reason.

"You are going to be spanked," Father said, "but you have a right to know why." His reasons were so overwhelmingly logical that I could not resist the spanking.

I conceive of the mind as a computer, the most intricate and sensitive computer ever constructed. Nothing that is fed into that computer is ever totally forgotten. We think that we are creating new ideas, but in reality we are only compiling information that we have already absorbed. If that information is warped and self-centered, then your mind will follow the same configuration. But if your upbringing has known freedom tempered with discipline, your computer will provide a similar result.

Am I painting too saintly a picture of my parents? Perhaps, perhaps. I realize that no portrait is accurate unless it includes defects—a mole or a wart here, a weak chin there. It's possible I should put more stress on my father's temper, my mother's pessimism. And yet my eyes can see only their goodness.

To them I am eternally grateful. Their help and upbringing in one world helped prepare me for life in another world that proved totally different and ever challenging.

SATURDAY

I was awake long before the chapel bell clanged for the retreatants to arise. Five-thirty is normally the time I get up when I'm working, so the seven o'clock rising at Manresa was no problem for me. Also, it is easy to climb out of bed after you have slept well. My first night's sleep at Manresa was the most restful I had known in months.

I consulted the schedule and recognized that we would be having a busy Saturday:

7:30 A.M. Morning Prayers
7:45 Breakfast
8:45 Group Picture
9:00 Conference in Chapel
10:30 Rosary
11:00 Conference in Chapel
12:00 Examen of Conscience in Chapel
12:15 P.M. Lunch
12:45–1:30 Confessions in Chapel
3:00 Stations of the Cross
4:15 Conference in Chapel
5:45 Celebration of the Eucharist—Homily
6:30 Dinner
7:00 Talk at Shrine of Virgin Mary
8:15 Conference in Chapel

8:45 Benediction of Blessed Sacrament in Chapel
9:15 Night Prayers

Before the day's schedule began, I had time to study some of the literature I had collected and to learn more about Manresa Retreat House. The name comes from a little town in northeastern Spain. It was there that the newly converted St. Ignatius Loyola spent eleven months in 1522 praying in solitude and performing acts of charity. At Manresa, St. Ignatius later said, he had visions of Christ and Mary, and the experience inspired him to start writing his *Spiritual Exercises*, which through the centuries have guided millions of people in their search for God. At Manresa he is also said to have begun formulating an organization that would be called the Society of Jesus. It began in 1534, when St. Ignatius and six other Paris students knelt in prayer in a little Montmartre chapel.

Jesuit retreat houses all over the world have been named Manresa, just as the one in Azusa. A strange name, Azusa. There is a legend that it came from city fathers who boasted that the community contained "everything from A to Z in the U.S.A." Alas, that is not true. According to the Manresa pamphlet, the native Shoshonean Indians named the place Azusa, meaning "Skunk-place." I can believe that, having sniffed the aroma of skunk before I fell asleep Friday night. However, another Indian expert believes Azusa means "His Grandmother, the Earth Goddess," which is a more romantic notion.

When the Franciscan fathers arrived in 1771, Azusa became part of the lands of the nearby Mission San Gabriel. Later Rancho Azusa was owned by a Mexican trader, an English adventurer, and finally an American banker whose daughter built the Norman château in 1932. The house and property, including a

large Roman pool, was acquired in 1947 by the Jesuits
for use as a retreat. That was the year when I first
came to Manresa.

So much for history.

After morning prayers, we retreatants enjoyed a
hearty breakfast of orange juice, cereal, bacon and
eggs, toast and coffee. It was our first silent meal, and
we quickly learned to pass the serving dishes with
smiles and inquiring expressions which could be inter-
preted as "Would you like some more eggs?" or "Another piece of toast?" I watched apprehensively as
David struggled to cut the bacon with his knife and
fork and lift a bite to his mouth. I wanted to tell him
to use his hands, but I didn't.

We were joined at breakfast by Father Bernard Basset, S.J. Not in person, but on tape cassettes that were
played at every meal. He proved to be a delightfully
stimulating companion, an Englishman of rare humor
and insight.

Father Basset remarked that he had conducted hundreds of retreats over twenty-five years, and added that
"Silence itself is not the retreat; what we need is to be
recollected. All of us lead today such very, very hurried and hectic lives. I don't know how you survive;
I'm nearly a nervous wreck after a month in the
States. . . . The pressure of our work today, the pressure of life itself, and all this commuting, traffic jams,
et cetera, means that if you're not careful, you almost
stop being human. You've got to collect yourself
where you've got scattered and dissipated over many
things. It's not a sin—but it's foolish. All the great
poets and all the great saints and all the great philosophers have known this: that if I don't keep quiet a little in my life, I become trivial."

One of the morning conferences was led by Father

O'Mara, another stouthearted Irishman, somewhat older than Father O'Gara, still vigorous, with an obvious interest in the sports world. He told of watching the PGA tournament on television and how Andy North needed a bogey to win. All that stood between him and victory was a 42-inch putt, a distance he later admitted "seemed like the Grand Canyon." Twice he walked up to the ball, twice he retreated. A third time he addressed the ball—and sank it.

"Golf pros pay great attention to details," said Father O'Mara. "They are careful how they plant their feet, how they position their wrists, their elbows, how they eye the ball. Most of all, they preserve their concentration. They *have* to concentrate when they're driving down those avenues of people. They realize the need for tremendous discipline.

"My advice to you is: take a tip from the pros. Retreats have been my business for many years, and I know how you can apply the lessons of golf. Your stance is important. You need not be in a kneeling position; you can communicate with God when you are sitting or walking around the grounds. But you have to be *alone* with Him. That does not mean that you will be lonesome; you will be *alone*.

"You'll notice that the golf pros practice courtesy. When another player is addressing the ball, they do nothing to distract him. The same is true in a retreat. Your friends have given up weekends with their families to be here. Respect that. Instead of facing a golf ball, they are trying to keep their minds on God. Don't be a distraction."

Father O'Mara mentioned a recent article in the Los Angeles *Times* about the Big Bang, the explosion that scientists speculate was the inception of the earth.

"Do we know how this world got started? We know that it's not eternal. What was its origin? That kind of search occupies everyone's mind nowadays. It's the reason for the interest in UFOs and the popularity of films like *Star Wars* and *Close Encounters.* How did we get here? Here at this retreat we are going to try to find out.

"To use another expression that has been popular, what are your roots? One American was so curious that he traveled back seven generations to trace his family's origins in Africa. He was consumed by questions that concern us all: Who am I? How did I get started?

"I found out when I spent some time in Rome. I had the privilege of saying Mass several times in St. Peter's. One day as I was preparing myself in the sacristy, I looked up and saw a list of the people who were buried in St. Peter's. There was a long list, perhaps two hundred and fifty, extending from John XXIII all the way back to Peter. I thought to myself, 'Here is the connection all the way back to Peter and from him to Christ and from Him to God. These are *my* roots,' I realized.

"Think about *your* roots this weekend. You will be able to walk with dignity and with purpose when you know where you came from and where you are going."

A year before he died, my brother Pedro sent me a genealogy of the Montalban family. The first Montalbans lived in France, then Reinaldos de Montalban went to Spain in the early 1600s. His son was Alonso de Montalban, who married a Castilian girl and settled in Madrid. Later the family moved to Valladolid, and there my father was born. Because of their service to Spain, the Montalbans had been accorded a minor title, and the family coat of arms was ornamented with two golden dragons and two fleurs-de-lis, also of gold.

My uncle Pedro was a great influence on our lives. He was my mother's brother, and she was his favorite, perhaps because she was the youngest of thirteen children. As a priest, he not only performed the marriage ceremony for Mother and Father, he also baptized all four children. Uncle Pedro was transferred to Mexico, where he became noted for his valor. During the revolution he was with Father Cortes, who hid Alvaro Obregón and saved the life of the man who became President. Uncle Pedro had commanding presence and a basso profundo voice that could fill a cathedral; his Masses were like concerts.

It was because of Uncle Pedro that my family went to Mexico.

Grandmother Merino longed to see her son in the New World, and so Father used his savings to take her and Mother to Mexico. They remained for several months, and during the visit my brother Carlos was born, June of 1904. (He was baptized Jesus but adopted Carlos when he moved to the United States, where Jesus is not customary as a man's name.) My parents returned to Spain, and Pedro was born in Soria, January 1906. Again my grandmother yearned to see Uncle Pedro, and Father decided he would move her and his young family to Mexico.

Imagine the adventure for a young man and woman to leave their homeland and seek the unknown on another continent. That took courage. They arrived in Vera Cruz on June 6, 1906, accompanied by my aged grandmother and two young boys, and proceeded to Mexico City. There Father opened a store that offered "Articles for Gentlemen"; in other words, a men's shop. He was an enterprising man, and he was the first to bring an industrial Singer sewing machine to Mexico, using it to make men's suits.

Those were perilous times in Mexico. Revolutionary armies swept out one regime and brought in another, only to be de-

posed by another army. Fortunes were lost because each new
government printed its own money. My father once went to
bed a rich man, his suitcase stuffed with currency. He arose the
next morning a pauper, a new government having printed fresh
money.

They were violent times, too. During the tragic ten days of
February 1914, Mexico City was under siege. Bombs were being
fired from the citadel to the palace, and they landed in the
courtyard of the apartment building where my family lived, El
Seminario, the first apartment house in Mexico. Mother was
running for shelter with my sister, Carmen, a little more than a
year old, in her arms. A shell burst over Mother's head and she
fell to the ground. Miraculously, she and Carmen were unhurt.
The shell exploded in a perfect cone, splattering the walls with
shrapnel but not hitting the ground.

After the birth of Carmen in 1912, Mother had many miscarriages. She had given birth to another son between my two
brothers, and he had died in infancy; I suspect his death and
the miscarriages were due to the RH blood factor, which was
unknown in those years. Fortunately for me, my parents still
tried for another child, and I was born in Mexico City on No-
vember 25, 1920. A large baby—over nine pounds.

I remember almost nothing of my early years in Mexico City.
The milk wagon toy my sister bought me for Christmas, yes.
Very little else. I was five when we moved to Torreón, following the failure of my father's business. It was not his fault. His
clothing business had prospered after President Adolfo de la
Huerta awarded him a contract to make uniforms for the mail-
men. That led to a contract to uniform the Constitutionalist
Army, which proved to be Father's ruin. The Treasury Department guaranteed payment, but by the time Father had completed thousands of uniforms, the government had changed
once more. The new rulers of Mexico would not pay.

My parents had wearied of the chaos of life in the capital.

When Father received an offer to manage a dry goods store in Torreón, he decided to move his family there.

Torreón in the mid-1920s was a bustling city of 80,000 in the northern state of Coahuila. Principal industry: cotton. It was a new city that owed its existence to the railroad. Two older towns nearby had decided they didn't want the trains passing through, and so the tracks were laid ten miles away. Around the terminal arose Torreón, and it soon outgrew the two older towns.

We lived in a pleasant house on Avenida Morelos, which had a park in the middle planted with palm trees. How tall those trees seemed when I was a boy! How much they had shrunk when I returned there in later years.

I led an orderly life. I arose at seven and enjoyed a hearty breakfast—fruit, toast, coffee, French-style bread or *tortilla,* my favorite *huevos rancheros* with *chorizo* or perhaps a slice of *jamón serrano* plus refried beans on the side. The school bus arrived at eight and returned at twelve-thirty, when the whole family gathered for the big meal of the day. Father took a recess from the store, as did all the other merchants. I did some schoolwork, perhaps took a brief nap, then back to school from two-thirty to five. More homework in the evening, and when Father returned from work after eight we sat down to a light meal. A bowl of soup and bread. Hot chocolate and a sweet roll. How much more sensible than going to bed stuffed, as we do in the United States.

Sundays were always happy days for the family. After Mass we returned for the big midday meal, and Father always brought home some ice cream or special cookies for a treat. I remember those Sundays well. I remember, too, a large book that was always near the table in the living room. Not until I was older did I realize that it was a dictionary. Father was a stickler on semantics, and he insisted that his children choose the right words to express themselves. Whenever he detected a misused word, he reached for the dictionary and found the

right meaning. As a result, my brothers, my sister, and I grew
up with a respect for language.

"*Gachupin! Gachupin!*"
I remember hearing that taunting word from my earliest
years in school. I was a new boy in town, and I desperately
wanted to make friends. But the other boys laughed whenever I
spoke, and they called me a name I had never heard before. I
ran home and sobbed in my mother's arms.

My mother and father came from Castile, so naturally they
spoke Castilian Spanish. And their children did the same. In
Castilian the soft *c* before *e* or *i* is pronounced *th*. There is a
legend that King Philip V spoke with a lisp and all his cour-
tiers did the same so he would not be embarrassed. Not true. If
it were, Castilians would pronounce *s* as *th*, and they don't.

To the American ear, Castilian sounds strange, even effemi-
nate. To Mexicans when I was a boy, Castilian had another con-
notation: *gachupin*.

My mother explained that *gachupin* was the name the Mexican Indians gave to the conquistadores. It meant man-and-
beast, or centaur. The Indians had never seen horses before,
hence they were astonished by men astride four-legged animals.
Over the centuries *gachupin* was the name applied to the
Spanish in Mexico, and it was not always a compliment. Some
Mexicans used it as an epithet, expressing their anger against
conquistadores who plundered the Aztec gold and massacred
the population. No doubt there were villains among the in-
vaders, but there were good men as well.

As I grew up in Mexico, I continued hearing bad things
about Spain and the Spanish. I was confused and divided. Mexico was my home country, and I loved it from my gut. But
Spain had given me my parents; all my relatives still lived in
Spain. In order to love Mexico did I have to hate Spain? I
couldn't do it. Spain was too much a part of my heritage.

In time the stigma of *gachupin* was forgotten, and I was accepted. I made many good friends among my schoolmates, some of them with Spanish parents, most of them Indian. My parents never swayed me; they both believed strongly that an individual should be judged on his own character, not his blood, nor the shade of his skin. As I grew older, I noticed the resentment against the *gachupins* diminished, and now I believe Mexicans take equal pride in their Spanish and Indian heritages. I suspect that much of the antipathy was fostered by American historians who stressed the evils of the conquistadores in an effort to urge Mexico to cut the umbilical cord to Spain.

Language was not the only thing that made me different during my Mexican upbringing. My mother believed that boys should be dressed in the Spanish manner, and that meant short pants.

"But, Mama," I pleaded, "none of the other boys in school wear short pants!"

"Ah yes, and they look like dwarfs," she replied.

"They make fun of me. They call me a little baby."

"You are not a little baby, and you can prove it to them. Your brothers wore short pants, and you will wear short pants. Like a little gentleman."

And so I continued wearing short pants long after my legs had grown long and hairy. It is not easy to grow up in a country that has different customs from your own family's. The Montalbans differed from their neighbors not only in the matters of language and short vs. long pants for boys, but also in food, customs, the formality of our manners, and in other ways. I had to learn to withstand the taunts of my playmates.

My father taught me a good lesson one day. A Japanese dentist moved into the house next to ours, and I noticed how strange and alien he seemed. After work he enjoyed playing phonograph records from his native country. To my young ears the high, reedy sounds of the Japanese women singers seemed hilarious, and I imitated the sounds one evening.

"Now, Ricardo," my father said, "the dentist who lives next door is a man of culture. He finds beauty in the music that he plays, otherwise he wouldn't listen to it. Perhaps there is something lacking in you that you cannot understand the beauty in the music. Perhaps he should be laughing at you for your ignorance instead of you laughing at him. If you want to discover anything in life, you must be an adventurer. You must be willing and eager to seek new adventures in sounds, in tastes, in people and experiences. Then, and only then, will your life become enriched."

I was very young when my father told me that, but I have never forgotten his advice. It has permeated my whole life.

My first three years of school were spent at the Alfonso XIII Grammar School, then I attended Colegio de la Paz, conducted by nuns. I was a good student—in subjects that interested me. I enjoyed mathematics, grammar and logic, I disliked history and geography. I can't explain why, except that I was never comfortable in studies that required a lot of memorizing. For instance, I enjoyed botany, but I was terrible in chemistry. Why? I suppose because I loved learning about plants, but chemistry, although it was related to mathematics, called for much memorizing of elements and their relationships.

I read a great deal. My parents believed that children should not run wild, and I guess you might say that I was sheltered. Since I was by far the youngest child in the family, I had no one to play with, and hence I read. I loved adventure novels. A special favorite was James Oliver Curwood's *Nomads of the North*. At the time I was reading it, my sister, Carmen, was learning a piano piece, "Etude for the Black Keys," by Chopin. It's strange how the mind associates things. I cannot hear that Chopin étude without thinking of *Nomads of the North*. Another favorite author was Emilio Salgari, who wrote sword-rattling tales of pirates. I also enjoyed books on zoology, and I learned the Latin names of many species.

Athletics, yes. I was a pretty good soccer player, but my forte became frontennis. It is a game much like squash, played with a tennis-like racquet and a jai alai ball. It required great endurance and coordination, and I loved it. So much that I would arise at 3:30 A.M., run to a club my brother, Pedro, belonged to in Torreón, play a couple of games, and run home to shower before leaving for school.

Summer was a joyful time for me, since I spent two months with the Gurza family at their cattle ranch in the state of Durango. Don Emilio and his wife were almost like an uncle and aunt to me, and their son, Luis, who was my age, was my best friend. The days were full. Always there was something going on at the ranch—calf branding, sheep shearing, rounding up the strays. We swam in the ponds and climbed the mountains; I was such a good climber they called me The Goat.

Also, Luis and I played at fighting the bulls. They were female calves, really, but as big as their male cousins that were destined for bull rings throughout Mexico.

I dreamed of becoming a bullfighter. I suppose every Mexican boy does at one time or another. When I was a teen-ager, I became acquainted with Carlos Arruza, who was then just beginning his brilliant career as a bullfighter. Carlos and I had much in common, both of us being born in Mexico of Spanish parents. We played jai alai together, and I watched him dress for the bullfight at his hotel, then accompanied him to the ring. Afterward we strolled around the plaza at night, and I basked in the reflected glory.

My parents were alarmed that I might pursue my ambition to become a *torero*. They need not have worried. I soon realized I lacked the courage. It takes an immense amount of it to confront a thousand pounds of charging bull.

Those summers on the ranch refreshed my soul after a long year of study. Often I rode over the hills alone on horseback or went on solitary hikes. There is the expression, "to have your feet on the ground." To me it means more than being level-headed and stable. When I was alone with nature, a feeling of strength seemed to rise from the earth and enter my being. The silence was such that I could hear my innermost thoughts with remarkable clarity.

How I miss that today! The pursuit of an acting career requires almost constant talk, talk, talk. Is it any wonder that I cherish the blessed silence of a retreat?

There were many things to occupy a boy growing up in Mexico, including girls and movies.

In Mexico, as in every country, boys after a certain age are always thinking about girls. When I look back on the era of my youth, I can recognize that it was a very romantic period, perhaps overly so. But I think I preferred it that way. Maybe I'm just a corny guy; I'm sure a lot of today's generation will consider me so. But I can't help believing that life was more beautiful in a time when women were idealized and the ritual of courtship was a slow, sometimes painful but basically elegant social custom.

I was shy. I wanted to be like the other boys and have a "sweetheart," but I didn't know how to go about it. Every boy had a "sweetheart." That didn't mean they went out on dates; the girls were always chaperoned. But the boy had asked and the girl had agreed to be his sweetheart. Very romantic, if not very satisfying.

How do you get a sweetheart? You pick out a girl who seems attractive to you. You smile at her. If she smiles back, there is a chance. If she doesn't, forget it. You go to the girl's house, make friendly overtures. Perhaps she will even go for a walk around the block. Never alone, of course; always with her sisters or cousins. You might sit on the front steps of her house on a warm summer evening, talking about this and that.

You go to the local country club and she is there. You swim and tell jokes, play the guitar. Her eyes meet yours, but you don't dare ask her to be your sweetheart. You go home and write poetry. You pass by her house, not merely by chance. Perhaps, if the timing is right, you will see her passing before the light in the upstairs window. Your heart leaps.

The school dance. The girls sit on one side of the hall, the boys on the opposite side. The mothers on a third side. You summon your courage and walk straight across no-man's-land and ask her, "May I have this dance?" If she says no, your life is ruined. But she says yes, and your heart is pounding. You take her hand in yours and place your arm around her waist. Angels are singing, and the school gym becomes a palace.

Was it all a romantic illusion? Perhaps so, by today's standards. The pace is faster nowadays. But not, I fear, as enjoyable.

I also discovered movies.

There wasn't much in the way of amusement in a town like Torreón. So I naturally drifted toward the movies, and I was enthralled. There in the darkened cinema a whole new world opened for me. It was a world of beautiful people, shiny automobiles, and eye-filling vistas. American movies were shown in English with Spanish subtitles, and so I was able to absorb the tempo of American talk even if I didn't understand what was being said. I was overwhelmed by the elegant speech of John Barrymore; to me he was the epitome of a fine actor. Wallace Beery did not impress me. Many years later, when MGM permitted me to screen films every Thursday night to help improve my accent, I saw the movies of both actors again. To my surprise, I discovered that Wally Beery was an excellent actor, while Barrymore, despite his magnetic personality, seemingly could not do a scene without his hand in his pocket or a cigarette in his hand.

I developed crushes on Hollywood actresses. Greta Garbo overwhelmed me. I adored Ginger Rogers from the first time I saw her with Joe E. Brown in *The Tenderfoot* (it was titled *The Neophyte* in Mexico) when I was twelve years old.

Did I dream then of becoming an actor?

Perhaps, but I don't remember it as a driving ambition. Certainly I long remembered seeing Manolo Fabregas in *Dr. Fu Manchu,* and mentally I put myself in his place. I was doing some performing myself, but as a singer. People said that I had a remarkable soprano voice—better than Bobby Breen's. I was often called upon to sing in school programs and at receptions for visiting dignitaries, my sister, Carmen, playing the accompaniment on the piano. Singing came easily to me, and I enjoyed the appearances. I may have even nurtured a dream of becoming another Bobby Breen.

Alas, my career was destroyed in one devastating performance. The Spanish ambassador was paying a visit to Torreón, and I was chosen to sing for him. Carmen played the introduction to "La Partida," and I began my usual self-assured rendition. As I was reaching for a high note, my voice suddenly cracked. Laughter broke out, and I could barely finish the chorus before fleeing from the room. I never sang again until I was an adult. And even though I have sung hundreds of performances in films and onstage, I have never felt at ease. My computer of a brain simply will not deprogram that embarrassing performance before the Spanish ambassador.

"Good-bye, Mama. Good-bye, Papa."
"Good-bye, Ricardo. Be a good boy."
"Make us proud of you."
I gulped back the tears as the train pulled out of the Torreón station. I waved and waved to Mother and Father, who stood on the platform and also struggled not to cry. They wanted my departure to school in Mexico City to be a happy time. But of course they could not avoid the sorrow of bidding farewell to their youngest son for the first time. Nor could I ignore the trepidation over leaving home. I was fourteen years old.

Soon excitement overcame the fear as I settled in my seat and watched the countryside race by. Because of my brother Pedro, I was going off to school in Mexico City, to study with the Maristas priests. I felt sad to leave my family and all the friends I had made in school. But Pedro had convinced me that this was the right thing to do. Only by acquiring a solid education could I achieve my potential in life. I tried to remember his words instead of thinking of my favorite girl, my comfortable room at home, the faces of my mother and father, whom I would not see for a year.

I was dazzled by the capital. Such movement, so many people, so much noise! I had arrived two weeks before the start of school, and I was taken into the home of two dear friends of my parents—he was Justo Merino, a distant cousin of Mother's. They had two children of their own, and the warmth of their home atmosphere helped ease the transition to boarding school. They took me to meet the principal and look over the school, and then I was left all alone.

The first night at school was the longest of my life. I lay awake for hours in the long dormitory with beds along each wall. I had my own domain, a few square feet that contained my bed and all my belongings. No more the luxury of my own room, where I could retire to my private thoughts. Now I had to share space with a couple dozen other boys, and I listened to their sleeping noises until finally I, too, fell asleep.

"All right, young men. Time to rise and see the new day that God has given us."

I felt as if I had just fallen into slumber when a smiling priest was urging me to get out of bed. Half asleep, I stumbled off to the showers, donned the school uniform, and marched off to breakfast with the other boys. Life was like that at the school: organized, disciplined. Necessarily so, since the priests had charge of the education of boys from all over Mexico, from every kind of background. Without a strong hand, the school would have been chaotic. And the Maristas brothers were strong. The headmaster was a Basque, one of the toughest hombres I have ever known. As young and agile as we boys were, we could never beat him at handball. Nor at anything else. He was strong in everything, especially the meting out of punishment. Yet I never felt oppressed. Behind that stern discipline I could feel a sense of love. So I never rebelled.

Not that I didn't get into trouble. Like any young person, I wanted to be accepted by my peers, to be "one of the boys." This, I learned, could be both foolish and dangerous.

Children can be cruel to anyone who seems different. I discovered that at an early age. And I saw it happen again with a boy at our school, a Mexican who had lived in the United States. His name was Manuel, and his manner was strange to the other boys; they considered him a sissy. They taunted him, but he tried to ignore their abuse. That made the boys angry.

"We want you to beat him up," the ringleader told me.

"Why should I fight him?" I replied. "He hasn't done anything to me."

"Never mind. He's a sissy, and we're going to show him up."

I continued my protest, but the other boys were unrelenting. Now it became a matter of machismo. I had to fight Manuel to show that I was strong and fearless, a real man. That's what they tried to convince me, but I still had doubts. They picked the time—during the recreation hour after dinner. We were all playing basketball, and two of the boys pushed me into Manuel. At once the cries went up for a fight, and my misplaced macho overcame my reason. I lifted my fists the way I had seen James Cagney do in the movies.

Wham! I felt a blow on my jaw. Sock! A crushing hit on my ear. I started flailing my fists, but Manuel merely danced around me. As I gazed at him bewilderedly, he landed another blow on my cheek. The other boys cheered for me, but the mismatch was obvious. When the headmaster rushed in to separate us, I was a bloody mess and Manuel was virtually untouched. Both of us were loaded with extra homework and required to stay within quarters for two weekends. We became good friends. I learned two painful but important lessons: never follow the crowd; nothing is solved by violence.

I learned to adjust to my new environment, and not merely

to adjust but to enjoy the experience. I found I could adapt easily to new situations, and my mind was stimulated by the teaching of the brothers. A new world of the intellect was opening up for me. But my stay at the Maristas school ended after one year. The government was undergoing a period of antagonism toward the Church, and all religious schools were ordered shut down.

Home to Torreón. I returned to the local school with no firm notion of what my destiny would be. My father tried to incline me toward the line of work he had pursued.

"Commerce is a noble profession," he explained. "I'm not sure if it will ever bring you wealth, but you will never lack food on your table. Commerce can be very rewarding—if you apply yourself. In other professions you can work very hard and see no results. But in commerce you will profit from your industry."

I was a dutiful son, and at Father's suggestion I enrolled at the Academi Comercial Treviño—business school. My goal: to become a certified public accountant.

No budding accountant was ever more miserable. I detested the tedium of adding up columns of figures all day, and I quit the commercial academy six months before graduation, much to my father's distress. Since I would not go to school, I would have to work, and I was enrolled as an apprentice at the dry goods store of Señor Fernando Gandara.

He was a Spaniard, a small, spare man but a giant in the dry goods world. His store was named Atoyac Textil, after an Aztec god, and Señor Gandara ran the place with an iron hand. He was quick to see the eagerness to learn on the part of his seventeen-year-old apprentice, and he gave me increasing responsibilities. I sold blouses and shirts to the customers, and measured out the yardage of material. Every morning I carried the previous day's receipts to the bank. I filled out orders for the traveling salesmen. When the cashier was absent, I took over the cash register. I developed a stock inventory system that

Señor Gandara told me twenty-five years later he still retained.
I arranged the merchandise and dusted off the showcases. All
this for forty pesos a month at a time when 3.60 pesos equaled
one American dollar.

It was absorbing work but unsatisfying. Fortunately, my
brother Carlos came to my rescue.

"A retreat is a school," said Father O'Gara at the
Saturday morning conference in the chapel. "In every
school there is an examination. Who gives the examination? You do. Examine your conscience, look deep
within your soul, and determine if you are following
the kind of life that God meant for you."

I can remember retreats from my years at boarding
school in Mexico City. We didn't leave the school;
the boys simply observed twenty-four hours of silence,
during which we were to receive spiritual enrichment.
I'm not sure it worked. Teen-age boys don't really
have much appreciation of silence.

Not until I moved to California and became en-
gaged in an acting career did I fully realize the value
of retreats. I have experienced several kinds. I have
been on retreats with doctors and with lawyers; it
seems to me that a weekend with more varied individ-
uals, like the one at Manresa, is preferable. I have also
been on husband-and-wife retreats, but have found
them less successful. The husband seems to keep eye-
ing the wife, thinking, "*I* understand; I hope she's
getting the message." And the wife is thinking the
same thing.

Father O'Gara had advised us at the beginning of
our retreat: "This is a working weekend. You would
be wise to take notes of things you want to remember.
Keeping a diary is a good idea. And use the library; it

is filled with a vast amount of inspiration and enlight-
enment."

The library was a cool, inviting haven filled with
valuable books and precious silence. From the oak
floor to the vaulted ceiling, books lined the walls, and
I marveled at how much had been written about
Christianity and the Church.

I wanted to know more about the institution of the
retreat, and I hunted through the shelves and cabinets
until I found the Catholic Encyclopedia.

"A retreat is a prolonged and intensified engagement in spiritual exercises in a setting secluded from
the ordinary affairs of secular life," I read.

Christ set the pattern, as recorded by Matthew:
"Then Jesus was led up by the Spirit into the wilder-
ness to be tempted by the devil. And he fasted forty
days and forty nights, and afterward he was hungry.
And the tempter came to him and said, 'If you are the
Son of God, command these stones to become loaves
of bread.' But he answered, 'It is written, "Man shall
not live by bread alone, but by every word that proceeds from the mouth of God." ' "

Christ advised his disciples: "Come away by yourselves to a lonely place, and rest awhile." The first
Christian retreat came after the Ascension, when the
disciples devoted themselves to prayer in preparation
for the Holy Spirit.

The early priests and desert monks sought solitude,
and Pope Gregory I in the sixth century advised those
in authority to interrupt "the clamor of earthly activity." Down through history monks have observed Lent
as a period of retreat. St. Ignatius provided the basis
for the modern retreat with his *Spiritual Exercises*,
and the practice spread through the Catholic world in

the seventeenth and eighteenth centuries. Pope Pius XI made Ignatius the patron of retreats.

What a wonderful communion with God the retreat can be! I felt the same way as I did when I had a reunion with my friend Max in Mexico City. When I saw him, it was as though we had just met the day before; we picked up our friendship immediately. Yet I never write him, I don't even send him a postcard. Sometimes a year or two passes before we meet again.

On a retreat I have the same feeling of renewed acquaintance with God. Of course I pay Him a visit every Sunday, but it's not the same as the sustained, direct, unencumbered communication on a retreat.

The Jesuits fed us well. The menu for Saturday lunch consisted of chili and beans, boiled spinach, cole slaw, corn bread, apple sauce, and cookies. The food was simple, well prepared, and tasteful, though perilous for an actor. The exercise had been more spiritual than physical, yet my appetite was large.

At three o'clock in the afternoon the retreatants met in front of the main house for the ceremony of the Stations of the Cross. There were fourteen shrines scattered under the towering oaks and pines, each representing significant places on the last journey of Christ. Each of us had a retreat prayer book, and we followed Father Brannon from one station to the next, hearing him describe the route and responding with prayers.

David was late. He often was the last to arrive, and he hobbled into view as the rest of us were standing before the Second Station. He stood at the top of a slight rise, as if contemplating whether he could descend without taking a tumble. We watched him, and I'm sure everyone shared my apprehension. Should I try to help him down the slope? Would he resent the

assistance? Before any of us could act, he started toward us, step after painful step. He made it safely,
with his customary smile.

During the afternoon we had an hour of solitude. It
was a good time to sit under a flowering jacaranda and
contemplate. I pondered the curious chain of events
that brought me to the United States, to my profession, to my marriage. But for a number of seemingly
casual happenings, I might now be manager of the
Atoyac Textil store in Torreón, Mexico. Did it all
happen by chance? I don't think so.

During my childhood I was blessed with not one but two
mothers—and three fathers. How could that be? I arrived late
in my parents' married life, and I had brothers who were fourteen and fifteen years older than I, and a sister who was eight
years older. I was more like their own child than a brother.

My oldest memory concerns the generosity of my sister, Carmen. It is the only memory I have of Mexico City, from which
we moved when I was five. I can still picture a toy I loved, a
milk wagon painted red, with thick spoked wheels, and a beautiful white horse pulling it. I saw it in the window of a toy
store near our house, and every day I went to stare at it. On
Christmas morning I found the milk wagon sitting on my bed.
Carmen had saved her tiny allowance for a year, never permit-
ting herself a piece of candy, so she could buy the gift for me.

My brother Carlos, being the oldest in the family, was the
first to leave home. Pedro, who stayed in Torreón, thought I
would get a better education by going to the capital, and so he
paid for me to take the train and enroll with the Maristas
priests' school. Years later when I returned to Mexico City to
become an actor, Pedro and his wife took me into their own
home.

My brother Carlos first brought me to the United States. I
had finished high school and was working in Torreón as ap-

prentice in a dry goods store. Carlos realized that I was unhappy with my work, and he believed an education in the
United States would prepare me for something better. Carlos
himself had moved to Los Angeles, and he suggested to my parents that I go live with him and attend school there. Regret-
fully, Mother and Father agreed.

Carlos drove from Los Angeles to Torreón to get me, arriving
in a beautiful black Buick coupé with white sidewall tires. He
parked the car in the gas station down the street during the
week he remained in Torreón, and every night I went to admire it. I ran my hand along the shiny black fender and said,
"This is the car that will take me to the United States!" My
head was filled with prospects of adventure. I felt as if I knew
California already, because of the movies. Perhaps I could even
see the inside of a movie studio. I might even be able to catch a
glance of Fred Astaire. Or Mickey Rooney. Or Deanna Durbin.
It would be like entering a dream world.

The sadness of leaving my parents was counterbalanced by
the thrill of approaching the country I had dreamed about. As
we drove along the bumpy Mexican roads, Carlos filled me
with tales of his adventures in Hollywood. He had gone there
in the mid-1930s, and his warm, outgoing personality made him
a favorite with studio people. Carlos was an excellent dancer,
and he doubled for Warner Baxter in tango scenes of *Under
the Pampas Moon* and performed some of the long shots for
George Raft in *Rhumba*, dancing with Carole Lombard. He
also helped stage the "Carioca" number in *Flying Down to Rio*
and acted in Spanish language films that were being made at
Fox in those years. Carlos grew tired of the precarious studio
life and decided to introduce Mexican beer to America. He
made an arrangement with the Carta Blanca brewery to act as
its representative in California, and he started to sell the product. He found allies among his movie star friends. When Joan
Crawford, Buster Keaton, Laurel and Hardy, Jean Harlow, and
other stars went to stylish restaurants and night clubs, they or-

dered Carta Blanca beer. Usually the establishments had none, and they placed orders with Carlos the next day.

Our journey brought us to the Rio Grande, and we crossed the border into Texas. At last I was in the United States! And soon I realized once more what it was like to be different.

As we drove westward along the long, straight highway, Carlos noticed the temperature gauge climbing. "Better stop and get some water at that gas station up there," he said. "I see a diner, too. Maybe we can get some chili. It's a Texas dish, very tasty."

He drove the Buick into the station, asked the attendant to fill it up with gasoline and check the water. Carlos and I got out of the car and started crunching across the graveled driveway toward the diner. Suddenly Carlos scowled and halted in his steps. He turned around and started leading me back to the car. "Let's go," he said.

"What's the matter?" I asked. "The sign says they have chili."

"We'll find a better place," my brother said.

Then I turned back and saw what had dissuaded him. It was a sign:

NO DOGS OR MEXICANS ALLOWED

As we continued along the highway, my mind was in a turmoil. I couldn't believe what I had seen. To me America had always seemed the land of freedom, where men and women of all races and backgrounds could live in liberty. Now I arrived here and saw that ugly sign!

My brother sensed my consternation and tried to assuage the hurt.

"Do not be upset, Ricardo," he said. "What you saw was the evidence of one man's prejudice. He cannot help it. He was brought up to hate Mexicans. You will find more of that in the United States, but you will find a great deal that is good. You in your small way can do something to erase that hate. By setting a good example. By loving."

It was hard for me to grasp. Why should I, a stranger from another country, be unwelcome in a roadside diner? Fortunately, the teachings of the Maristas priests were still fresh in my mind. "Hate the sin but love the sinner," they had taught me. If I had not remembered that, perhaps I would have become an angry militant, railing against such injustice. But, no. It was necessary for me to hate the sin of prejudice but love the person who was the victim of that sin. The greatest weapon against hatred is love.

I understand the militancy, the anger, the violence that minority people have evidenced in response to injustice. I understand it, but I can't join it. I have lost my temper on occasion, and I dislike the loss of logic. Rather than thinking negatively, I prefer the positivism of love.

I am writing now in the maturity of my years. Such thoughts did not come easily to that hurt young man riding along that endless highway on the route to California.

Hollywood was everything I had dreamed as a boy watching movies in Mexico. I felt as if I were visiting a strange and beautiful world as my brother drove his Buick down Hollywood Boulevard, past the fabulous Grauman's Chinese Theater. Everywhere I looked there were pleasures for the senses. Just to go to a drive-in eating place was a delight, especially to order a strawberry soda or a hamburger. Or to go to a skating rink! I had skated on the sidewalk in Torreón, but here in Hollywood they had a huge arena with a hardwood floor to skate upon, shimmering lights and organ music to add to the mood, and dozens of beautiful girls.

Every day was a new discovery. To walk along Gower Gulch and see the real, authentic cowboys in their chaps and boots. To stand outside the gates of Paramount and RKO and watch the extras walking by—harem girls, legionnaires, musketeers. I walked along Hollywood Boulevard hoping I would recognize an actor I had seen in films, and sometimes I did.

My life was not totally devoted to enjoying the delights of a new land. My brother had brought me to the United States to get an education, and so I began my studies. Because my English was poor, I was enrolled at Belmont High School, near downtown Los Angeles. It was a long distance from where my brother lived, on Kilkea Drive near Hollywood, and I spent a couple of hours on the bus going each way. Belmont High was like a Tower of Babel. It was designed for students to whom English was a second language, and I became acquainted with Mexicans, Italians (we could understand each other by speaking slowly), Greeks, Japanese, Chinese, Koreans, and others. After three months at Belmont, I passed the language test, and I was allowed to enroll at Fairfax High, not far from my brother's house.

I made more good friends at Fairfax. Many of them invited me into their homes, and I began to notice differences. With some of my friends, their home atmosphere was very much like mine in Torreón. The food was spicy and aromatic, and there was an unmistakable air of respect by the children for their parents. In other homes, the children talked back to their parents —it was shocking for me to hear—and the food was incredibly bland. For example, a salad of a banana on a bed of lettuce, smothered in mayonnaise! Later I realized the difference between the two sets of families. The ones with tasteful, spicy food were Jewish, the others were not.

Being welcomed into the homes helped assuage the hurt that still remained from seeing that ugly sign in the Texas diner. At both Belmont and Fairfax, students seemed to accept you as a human being, no matter how accented was your English or how slanted your eyes. But I discovered that attitude did not extend throughout Los Angeles.

My brother believed I had to earn my education, and so on weekends I helped load and deliver cases of beer with Carlos's assistant, whose name was Juan. He and I became friends, and one day I suggested that we go together to a dance hall in downtown Los Angeles. I remembered seeing Barbara Stanwyck in a movie about a dance hall girl, *Ten Cents a Dance*, and I was curious to see what one of those places looked like.

"Okay, Ricardo," said Juan, "let's go."

We took the beer truck downtown and parked it on Seventh Street. Both of us had put on our sharpest outfits, and we were certain that the hostesses would be clamoring to dance with us. We climbed the stairs to the second-floor ballroom and walked to the entrance. A burly man in uniform stood in our way.

"Wait a minute, you guys," he said. "Are you Mexicans?"

I looked at Juan with perplexity. He replied, "Yes, we are."

"No Mexicans allowed," the guard answered.

"But why?" I asked.

"You guys start too many fights," was the answer.

"But—" I started to protest, but Juan took my arm.

"That's all right, Ricardo," Juan said. "We'll go."

I was hurt and confused as I followed him down the stairs. "But why—why?" I asked.

"It's just one of those things," Juan said. "You can't do anything about it."

It still made no sense to me. How could this happen in a city whose name was Los Angeles, which Mexicans had settled long before anyone else arrived, which had streets named Alvarado, Sepulveda, Pico, Santa Monica, Figueroa? It seemed very sad.

The studies at Fairfax High seemed very easy to me after Mexico. I took only five subjects, compared to ten when I was in school at home. I got mostly A's and B's, and possibly I had an advantage by being older than the other students—I was eighteen. Because of the year I had spent in the commercial academy I did not have enough credits for college, hence I had to take some required subjects. My English was improving, but it still needed help, and my counselor advised me to take public speaking. This proved a fateful move in my life, for it led to my introduction to acting.

The teacher of public speaking was a warm, wonderful lady of Armenian extraction, Araxi Jamgochian. She was also the drama teacher. Perhaps she had trouble finding enough boys to appear in the plays. Or maybe she saw some well-hidden talent that needed to be nurtured. At any rate, she urged me to come out for the school play, *The Whole Town's Talking*, by Anita Loos. I hadn't forgotten the pleasure I received watching plays and movies in Torreón. I accepted.

I had a small role, but the experience of being onstage nevertheless overwhelmed me. I was still shy, especially in a land where I was unsure of the language. Yet onstage I discarded my identity and became someone else. I was the character in the play, and I need not conceive of things to say because the playwright had already provided them. It was a fascinating experience, like being a guest at a masked ball and losing your own personality behind the artifice of a mask.

Apparently I performed adequately in the play, because Miss Jamgochian next cast me in the leading role of *Tovarich*, the role that Charles Boyer performed in the movie. Now I felt the responsibility not only to provide an entertaining two hours for the audience, but also to aid and support my fellow players. My eighteen-year-old mind couldn't comprehend the enormity of it all, but I felt I was on the threshhold of something limitless and wonderful, something I wanted desperately to pursue.

In those years talent scouts for the movie studios went everywhere in search of prospects, even high school plays. To my astonishment, a scout from MGM telephoned me that he had seen my performance in *Tovarich* and would like me to come to the studio for a screen test. I breathlessly reported the news to my brother Carlos.

"That's very nice, Ricardo," said Carlos, who was wise in the ways of the studios. "But don't forget what you came to the country for."

"To get an education, yes," I said. "But how can I pass up this chance? They want to give me a screen test!"

"Do you know how many screen tests MGM gives every week? Listen, my brother, if you have the talent, they will ask you again. It is more important for you to go to college and prepare yourself for a line of work."

"But, Carlos—"

"I tell you what, Ricardo. I am going to New York to introduce the beer there. I will take you along, and you can stay out of school for six months. Perhaps you can find some acting to do there, so you can find out if that is what you truly want to do. But then I think you should go back to school."

I agreed to the compact, bargaining for six months of freedom to pursue my new passion. And of course I never went to school again.

Hollywood was what I imagined it would be. I was totally unprepared for New York.

It was like visiting the city of the future, or a vast metropolis on another planet. I could scarcely believe the immensity of the place, the excitement of the streets, the vitality of the people. I walked along Fifth Avenue and was awed by the women in elegant frocks and white gloves, the men in cutaways, carnation in the buttonhole, canes swinging jauntily. I walked to Times Square and strolled through the theater district. The marquees advertised Tallulah Bankhead in *The Little Foxes*, Olsen and Johnson in *Hellzapoppin*, Ethel Barrymore in *The Corn Is Green*, Alfred Lunt and Lynn Fontanne in *There Shall Be No Night*, Vincent Price in *Angel Street*, Gene Kelly in *Pal Joey*. I watched all of them from the balconies, and was dazzled.

My brother and his wife Mary lived at 110 West Fifty-fifth Street, between Sixth and Seventh avenues, and that was a fine location to start my walks through Manhattan. I went everywhere. Just strolling down the streets was entertainment in itself; there was always something to see that was fascinating and exciting. I loved to walk through Central Park and watch the sailors rowing boats. One of my biggest enjoyments was to go to Harlem in the evening and listen to the pulsating jazz.

Carlos was a dedicated salesman as well as a personable one, and he soon introduced Carta Blanca beer to "21," The Stork Club, El Morocco, Toots Shor's, and other fashionable places in New York. (Later, after Carlos had helped make the beer popular in America, the brewery decided it didn't need him anymore. I have not been able to enjoy Carta Blanca since then.)

Mary, Carlos's wife, had become acquainted with casting agents and other people in show business, and it was with her help that I started acting professionally. One day Carlos called me and said, "Well, my brother, how would you like to act in a movie? Mary has arranged it."

"Are you kidding me?" I said. "A real movie?"

"Well, sort of."

"What do you mean—'sort of'?"

"Have you seen those juke boxes where you put in a dime and you get a song on a movie screen?"

"Yes."

"That's it. They need some extras to listen to the songs while they're filmed."

It was a start. At least I was being paid as an actor for the first time in my life—forty-five dollars a week! The work wasn't hard. All I had to do was listen rapturously as Gertrude Neisen sang "My Man." I did several of them until—just as in the Ruby Keeler musicals—I got my big break.

The company had filmed a short with Gus Van singing "The Latin from Staten Island," but something went wrong with the camera. The producer decided to reshoot the number using the same sound track with a younger man. I was chosen!

I had been in New York only a few weeks and already I was starring in a movie! No matter that it was only a three-minute movie that would appear in bars and bowling alleys. This was my big chance.

The scene was meant to be the Staten Island ferry, and I was supposed to regale my listeners with the song about my Latin sweetheart. I gave it all I had, which was necessary because I was mouthing to the voice of a singer three times my age.

A couple of weeks later, the company informed me of the world premiere of my starring debut. It would be installed in the Hurricane Bar in midtown Manhattan. Carlos, his wife, Mary, and I got all dressed up and took a taxi to the Hurricane Bar. I eagerly searched the juke box and there it was: Ricardo singing "The Latin from Staten Island." No last name, just "Ricardo." Unfortunately, you couldn't select the number you wanted; you had to keep feeding the machine dimes until it came along in sequence. So I sat down at the bar and waited.

Carlos and Mary took stools at my right. To the left was a sailor. "Bartender, I'll have a shot of rye, a glass of beer, and a shot of bourbon," he ordered. I watched in awe as the sailor slugged down the rye, drank half of the beer, and emptied the bourbon shot glass. Then he took from his pocket half a lemon and a salt cellar, salted the lemon and sucked it.

Curiosity overcame me. "Pardon me, sir," I said, "but why do you suck the lemon?"

"So I won't get drunk," he said flatly. He repeated the ritual two more times, and I suspected that the lemon was not fulfilling its purpose.

Finally the title flashed on the juke box screen: "Ricardo Sings 'The Latin from Staten Island.'" I stared at the screen in wonder, not noticing that the sailor was glancing at it and then at me. When the number finished, Mary kissed me and Carlos patted me on the back. "You were marvelous, Ricardo," they said.

The sailor continued staring. "Hey, buddy, was that you?" he asked.

"Yes," I replied proudly.

"Brother, do you stink!" he said, pocketing his lemon and lurching out the door.

It was my introduction to New York critics.

Through Mary's connections, I managed to acquire an agency, Lyman and Chamberlain Brown. It had once been important in the theatrical world, but I gathered that the partners no longer wielded much influence. Why else would they take as a client a nineteen-year-old Mexican with a pronounced accent and no more experience than appearing in juke box movies?

One night after attending the theater, I stopped by Lindy's, where I had learned that the Broadway crowd gathered. I encountered one of the partners of the agency, Mr. Lyman, who invited me to sit at his table and have some coffee. As I was telling him my enthusiasm for the evening's play, we were interrupted by a telephone call for Mr. Lyman. When he returned to the table, he said, "Ricardo, I've got an idea. Come with me."

As we rode along Sixth Avenue in the taxi, he explained to me, "We are going to see Tallulah Bankhead at the Hotel Pierre."

"At this hour?" I said, glancing at my watch. It was 1:30 A.M.

"It doesn't matter with Talloo. Now I want to prepare you, Ricardo. I know you're an innocent boy from Mexico. So I don't want you to be shocked by what you may see or hear."

His admonition made me wonder what I was getting into. My fears were reinforced when the door to the hotel suite opened. I heard a string of expletives and gazed down at the hungry face of a half-grown lion. The expletives came from Miss Bankhead. The lion belonged to her, and it roamed the suite in defiance of a hotel edict against all pets.

Mr. Lyman introduced me, but that didn't interrupt Miss Bankhead's tirade. As far as I could gather, the object of her wrath was a young actor who could not remember his lines. She was occupying her summer by appearing in outlying theaters in an old play, *Her Cardboard Lover*. Her current engagement was at the Cedarhurst Theater on Long Island, and she claimed that night's performance had been ruined by the actor who played a minor but essential role as the croupier.

"The bastard froze, right onstage," Miss Bankhead ranted. "Couldn't remember a goddamn line! What could I do? I finally pushed him off the bloody stage. The entire first act was ruined—RUINED!"

Mr. Lyman commiserated with her until she calmed down a bit, and then he suggested, "How about having Ricardo play the role?"

Miss Bankhead looked at me for the first time. I was extremely nervous, especially since her lion was chewing holes in my brand-new shoes.

"This boy is an actor?" she asked.

"Certainly," Mr. Lyman said. "He's been appearing in some movies, but he's available to go right into the play."

"All right, I'll take him," she said. Then she fixed her eyes on me. "But if you forget your lines, young man, I'll have you boiled in oil."

I took a copy of the play home with me, and I never slept. I read the play over and over again, trying to imprint the croupier's lines into my mind. But another sentence kept interceding: "If you forget your lines, young man, I'll have you boiled in oil."

The next day I took the subway out to Long Island, arriving at the theater in plenty of time. I reported to the stage manager and inquired what time the rehearsal would be. He smiled indulgently.

"Ain't gonna be any rehearsal, young fella," said the stage manager. "When the time comes, I'll push you out on the stage. Your first line is, 'Yes, sir.' Just get the rest of the lines out, and when you finish, go upstage right and out the door." I was too embarrassed to ask him where upstage right was.

He took me by the arm and led me to a dressing room, where we encountered a young man in makeup and costume. "Oh, sorry, Michael," the stage manager said to the actor. "This fella is going to play your part tonight. Miss Bankhead's instructions."

We were left alone, the discharged croupier and his green replacement. As he started taking off the costume, he gazed at me with hatred in his eyes. The hate turned to contempt, and he snapped, "Don't you know that the first rule of makeup is to shave?" I looked in the mirror and was startled to see that I had a day's growth of beard. I had been so intent on learning the role that I had forgotten to shave.

"Curtain in five minutes!" The call made me shiver. I was wearing a costume still warm from its previous occupant, who had been fired for freezing onstage. Could I escape the same fate? I had no way of knowing. I had never had a professional job in the theater before.

"Curtain going up!"

I stood in the wings and watched the stage grow bright from the footlights. My heart pounded. I wanted to be back in Torreón, where I would be safe. Suddenly the stage manager gave me a little shove. "Good luck, boy," he said.

I walked onstage, squinting under the bright lights.

"Charles?"

"Yes, sir."

Ah, I managed to get the first line out. I gazed into the wings. Everyone in the cast was watching me. Including Tallulah Bankhead. My mind went totally blank.

But only for a brief second. The second line came to me, and it got a pleasant laugh. I even found my way to upstage right and made my exit.

After the performance, I was summoned to Miss Bankhead's dressing room. Her face was stern, and I feared for the worst.

"Young man, you will stay with us for the five-week tour," she announced. "I am pleased. This is almost like working in France, where even a small role like yours is portrayed with professionalism."

Miss Bankhead couldn't have been more helpful during the five-week tour. She gave me hints on how to improve my performance. When a New York newspaper asked her to do a photo spread on the Coney Island rides, she chose me to accompany her. And our relationship was never more than platonic.

Her Cardboard Lover helped me get roles in other summer theaters. I did a play starring Anita Louise, another with Anna Sten, then was cast with Elsa Maxwell in an old Somerset Maugham play, *Our Betters*. It was a slow, dated comedy that offered a good opportunity for the actor who played a gigolo in the third act. That was my role, and I came on to dance a conga with Miss Maxwell and convince her to stay in the country so she could not meet a deadline. The scene brought needed razzle-dazzle to the play, and I drew applause and good notices.

Also a screen test offer from MGM. The studio was planning to make *Tortilla Flat* with an all-Mexican cast, and I was being considered for the important part of Danny. I made the test with Lina Romay playing the role of Dolores Sweets Ramirez. We were told that the test was very successful. But Hollywood being what it was, our roles were cast with John Garfield and Hedy Lamarr. The other Mexicans in *Tortilla Flat* included Spencer Tracy, Ralph Morgan, Akim Tamiroff, and Sheldon Leonard. I was offered a smaller role in the film, but I could not accept.

"Ricardo, I have received a letter from Papa," my brother told me. "Mama is very sick, and she must have an operation. I think you should go home to Torreón."

"Please, God, make my mother well," I prayed before the altar of our parish church in Torreón. Although I was terribly worried about the outcome of Mother's operation, I felt a certain contentment to be back at home and speaking to God in familiar surroundings. I had gone to church faithfully during my two years in the United States, but somehow it wasn't the same. The stimulation of my everyday activities, first in Los Angeles and then in New York, occupied my thoughts, and religion seemed only a comfortable one-day observance. I felt none of the uplift that I had known as a boy in Mexico.

But once again in the silence of our little church in Torreón, I felt close to God. And I thanked Him when the doctors said Mother had come through the operation in fine condition and would be fully recovered in a few weeks.

Father talked to me about the future, and again he tried to convince me of the steadiness of a career in commerce. "I know the acting life seems very exciting and glamorous to you, Ricardo," he said. "But think of it as a living. Even if you have talent, you are not assured that someone will give you a job. Someday you will have a wife and children. How can you support them with the uncertainty of an actor's life? A man in business always knows he can earn a salary. Think about that, Ricardo."

It didn't take long for me to compare my job at the dry goods store and the life I had been introduced to in the theater. And so I again took leave of Torreón, but this time I headed south. The movie business was thriving in Mexico City, and I was certain that I could become a part of it.

My brother Pedro and his wife were living in Mexico City with their two daughters and Pedro's brother-in-law, and they graciously added me to their household. I had only one introduction to the movie world, but it was an important one. Carlos had told me that if I went to Mexico City I should look up his old school chum, Ramón Pereda, who had become one of Mexico's leading actors, and a producer and director as well.

"So you are the brother of Carlos Montalban!" Pereda said warmly. "And you want to be an actor?"

"Yes, sir," I admitted. "I had some experience in New York, you see."

"And you liked it?"

"Yes, sir!"

"Of course. It is a narcotic, the acting life. Well, perhaps I can help you, Ricardo. I will give you the names of some casting agents. And, Ricardo—"

"Yes, sir."

"Don't expect to get rich right away. Whenever your pocket is empty, come see my bookkeeper. He will issue you a check. And if you are hungry or just need someone to talk to, come have lunch with me. I eat at the same restaurant every day."

During the weeks of job hunting that followed, I accepted both his invitations. Even though Carlos and Mary sent me money and I lived in the most Spartan way, I still ran short of cash. Señor Pereda's bookkeeper came to my rescue.

Finally I landed a role. It was a parody of *The Three Musketeers*, starring a boyhood idol of mine, Cantinflas. I had a single, memorable line: "The carriage awaits."

Obviously my career could only rise from that point. And it did. I had another part that was somewhat larger, then I became involved in a project that provided one of the most profound influences in my life.

It was called *Hostages*, the story of Yugoslavian freedom fighters who tried to free citizens held hostage by the Nazis. A group of film makers had come to Mexico from Hollywood for the film. They included such actors as Howard daSilva, Frances Farmer, Leonid Kinsky, Howard Smith, Victor Kilian, and director Herbert Klein. All of them were oriented to the left, but I had no knowledge of it at the time. Even if I had, political matters were of faint interest to me.

The importance of *Hostages* in my life was that it introduced me to Seki Sano.

He was a dedicated Communist. A curious-looking man, short, certainly not handsome. He walked with a limp, yet he had an interesting, swaying walk, like a sailor who has been long at sea. Despite his lameness, he was a dynamic man. Deaf in one ear, he cocked his head when he listened. You could feel the intensity of his soul.

Seki Sano had been a musical prodigy in Japan. His family were well-to-do, and they bought him instruments to organize a symphony orchestra to play Western music. Japan had little acquaintance with Bach and Beethoven earlier in the century, and Seki Sano traveled throughout the islands to bring classical music to the masses. His orchestra was appearing in Yokohama when a tremendous earthquake struck. The concert hall was destroyed, along with the symphonic instruments.

The theater attracted Seki Sano. He was alarmed by the growing militarism in Japan, and he sought a way to speak out against it. So he wrote and produced plays attacking imperialism and the growing curtailment of freedom. That was his undoing. He defied orders to stop presenting plays critical of the regime. One night as he was walking home from the theater, he was attacked by a group of masked men. They drove him toward the sea, beat him relentlessly, and left him almost lifeless in a ravine. Next morning a fisherman's wife heard his groans, called her husband, and they took him to their boat. They nursed him back to life, but ever afterward he would be deaf in one ear and crippled in the left leg.

Realizing that his life was worthless in Japan, Seki Sano escaped to Russia, the only country that would accept him. He naturally gravitated to the theater. The great Konstantin Stanislavsky recognized his talent and made him an assistant at the Moscow Art Theater. The maestro even allowed Seki Sano to conduct rehearsals in his absence. After the Pearl Harbor attack, Seki Sano sought a way to help defeat his enemies, the militarists of Japan. His knowledge of the Japanese language at all levels was invaluable, and he offered his services to the United States in the effort to break the Japanese code. He was sent to Washington and reportedly was an important help in the eventual code breaking.

Seki Sano came to Mexico with the *Hostages* company and fell in love with the people. He was less pleased with the economic conditions he discovered, believing that the working classes were exploited by the moneyed few. As a devout Communist, he was determined to do something about it. He decided to repeat what he had done in Japan: present plays that exposed the injustices of the system. But he didn't go to the regular theaters of Mexico City. He decided he would teach members of the railroad workers' union to act.

I was immediately drawn by his magnetic personality. Even though I had the juvenile role in *Hostages*, he devoted much time to me, and his insights gave me a totally new view of acting.

When the movie was completed, I said to him, "Señor Sano, I would like very much to share your wisdom about acting. May I become your student?"

"No, no," he replied. "I am much too busy with the railroad workers."

"But I need you more than they do!" I protested. "They already have jobs. I am an unemployed actor. And I'm likely to remain that way unless somebody helps me learn the craft of acting."

He relented. He allowed me to enroll in his drama classes, and I found myself performing Gogol's *The Inspector General* with engineers, firemen, Pullman porters, and railroad switchmen. It was an unbelievably stimulating experience. I am sure that Seki Sano taught the Stanislavsky method, although his instruction was so subtle that I scarcely realized that I was being indoctrinated. He did not lean heavily on theory; he sought instead for the actor to bring his own interpretation out of his experience.

"Every moment that you convey to the audience must be original and fresh, totally new," he explained. "No matter how many times you perform a scene, make it the first time. Bring new forces, new thinking to it. Yes, you are playing the same character in the same scene, but find new undertones. Keep it alive, keep it different!"

It was not easy to transform his theory into practice, not when the railroad workers and I performed scenes again and again until we were weary of repeating the same words. But Seki Sano persisted.

"Look around you," he urged. "Notice the immense diversity in nature and in man's handiwork. You will be amazed at the beauty you can find."

I decided to try to put his teachings into practice. Each day my route to his classes was a tedious journey by streetcar and bus, a total bore, I thought. And then I followed his dictate to observe. As I was waiting for a streetcar near my brother's home, I gazed up at the wooden doors of a nearby house. I had never noticed the doors before, but now I saw that they were intricately carved in Aztec designs, the exquisite work of some forgotten artist. As I rode along the streets, I began to notice the colors. Growing up in Mexico, I had grown too accustomed to the bursts of bright reds, yellows, blues, and greens. Now I saw color everywhere.

And the faces. Mexico is a treasury of fascinating faces, ranging from the handsome, high-cheeked Indian to the narrow-faced, fine-boned Spaniard, and all gradations between. Some faces were compelling beautiful, others stark in their ugliness; all were worthy of study.

Seki Sano was always urging his students to observe, to absorb, to appreciate. One day in class he held up an egg and he asked, "What is this?" We answered the obvious.

"I know it is an egg," he replied, "but what does it mean to you?"

"Breakfast," said a railroad brakeman, evoking laughter.

"What else does it mean?" the teacher demanded.

"Life," answered a young woman who served meals on trains.

"That is better," Seki Sano commented. "Now you are start-ing to think. Look at the shape of the egg. Could a sculptor create anything that was as gracefully shaped and yet so func-tional? Look at the texture; the shell has pores. It breathes! In-side there is life. Think of the engineering of this masterpiece. If I take it with my finger and thumb at the poles and squeeze gradually, adding more and more pressure—it will not break. But if I squeeze it in the middle, look—" The egg crushed in his hand and fell into a dish. "You see, the arch gives it the strength to withstand pressure at the poles. It is a perfect de-sign, aimed at perpetuating the life that is inside. Think of the egg. Think of the other humble things you see every day, and marvel at their beauty."

Seki Sano and I became good friends; he seemed gratified with the seriousness I applied to acting. He also sought to in-struct me in another matter: politics.

"Aren't you appalled by all the poverty you see around you?" he asked. "The peons starve while the rich gorge themselves. That is not right, Ricardo."

I'll admit that his reasoning did hold some logic for me. I was also impressed by his accounts of the state of artists in the Soviet Union.

"In Russia you would not have to go from one casting office to another and have the doors slammed in your face," he said. "Anyone with talent such as yours would be recognized by the state as an artist. Your entire training would be subsidized by the state; you would learn under the finest teachers. And then you would be assured of work in the best repertory companies or in the film studios."

Again I was impressed, especially since he had admitted that I had talent. I might have been a prime candidate for conver-sion to his beliefs. And yet, and yet . . . Even though I felt a sympathy for the poor and the oppressed, something would not allow me to embrace communism. Perhaps it was my religious training, perhaps my suspicion that communism would not bring the freedom that its adherents predicted. Seki Sano soon recognized that I was a poor prospect for proselyting, and he continued devoting his efforts to the railroad workers. Fortunately for me, his disappointment did not destroy the relationship between teacher and student, and he remained a dear friend.

Hostages was unsuccessful, but it brought more attention to me as an actor. A topflight producer, Francisco Cabrera, offered to test me for the important role of a gypsy bullfighter in *Santa*, a remake of a classic story that had been made as a silent film and as an early talkie. As director Cabrera had brought from Hollywood Norman Foster, a former actor who had directed *Mr. Moto* and *Charlie Chan* movies as well as *Journey into Fear*, in which he was associated with Orson Welles. Foster was impressed with my Spanish background and my knowledge of gypsy and flamenco dialects, and he chose me for the role.

It may have been the most important step in my life. *Santa* made me a star in Mexico, and I worked with Norman Foster on four more films. The association also led to the one great love of my life.

I first saw her in a movie, *Alexander Graham Bell.* I was still a boy in Torreón; she was only thirteen years old. Loretta Young was the star, along with Don Ameche, and her three sisters in the film were played by her *real* sisters—Sally Blane, Polly Ann and Georgiana Young. I was absolutely entranced by the beauty and charm of Georgiana.

I saw her once again when I was attending Fairfax High School in Los Angeles. I borrowed my brother's car one Sunday to go to Mass at the Church of the Good Shepherd in Beverly Hills. Afterward I walked to the alley where I had parked the car. I glanced over and saw her in a car parked opposite mine. I tried desperately to catch her. No luck; she started the motor and drove away.

My heart pounded as I fumbled the key into the lock, started my car and slammed it into gear. I raced down Santa Monica Boulevard and happily caught up with her car. But just as I pulled alongside, she turned right. I was stuck in the left-hand lane. I speeded to the next block, turned right, and hurried around the block. But she was gone.

I have explained my relations with girls in Torreón. Very decorous, very proper. In Los Angeles and New York, I found myself gravitating to the same kind of girl. I had more respect for those who had been brought up with the same kind of conservative background that I had known. At first my dates were infrequent because I had to save up the allowance my brother gave me. Through friends I met South American girls who boarded at Immaculate Heart College. I also dated girls at Fairfax High School.

One of them was Millie Cohen. I was crazy about her, and I saved my money for a couple of weeks so I could take her out. Carlos loaned me his new car, a beautiful LaSalle coupé, and gave me a pair of tickets to the "Lux Radio Theater." I drove Millie to the theater on Vine Street, convinced that I was going to make a real impression on her. Carole Lombard was the star of the broadcast.

I confidently put my arm around Millie's shoulder as the broadcast began. Then a man with a mustache took the empty seat next to Millie. It was Clark Gable. I didn't stand a chance. Millie Cohen could talk only about Clark Gable for the remainder of the evening.

When I became a film actor in Mexico, I had more opportunity for acquaintance with women. Naturally, I grasped the opportunity. I was incurably romantic. Each new girl I met was the "love of my life." And indeed she was—for about three months. And then someone else came along.

I often rhapsodized about my latest amour to Norman Foster and his wife, Sally Blane, who had become good friends during the films he directed me in. "This is really the one," I insisted when I told them about a new girl.

"Oh, Ricardo, you always say that," Sally laughed. "But I don't think you're really serious. You go on having your little romances, but don't do anything drastic until you meet my sister."

"Who is your sister?" I asked.

"I'll show you." Sally picked a copy of *Harper's Bazaar* from the coffee table and opened it to a fashion spread. There she was! The girl in *Alexander Graham Bell*. The one I had tried to follow after Mass at the Church of the Good Shepherd.

"That's your sister?" I asked.

"Of course. Georgiana, the baby of our family."

"But what is she doing in this magazine?"

"My mother went to New York for some decorating commissions. She took Georgiana along. Carmel Snow, the editor of *Harper's Bazaar*, saw her and wanted Georgiana to work for the magazine. Now Georgiana is the most popular fashion model in New York."

I was too shy to reveal that I had a crush on Sally's sister. Every week I went to a store that sold American magazines. I looked through all the fashion magazines and bought the ones that had photographs of Georgiana. I cut out the pictures and made a collection of them.

Sally decided to return to California for some shopping. Since I was between films, I decided to make the trip, too. I flew with a friend, an airline pilot, who asked me where I was going to stay.

"Oh, I'll get a hotel room somewhere," I said.

"Are you kidding?" he answered. "Didn't you know all the hotels are jammed because of the war? There are people sleeping in the lobbies. You'd better stay with us. The pilots have a special suite at the Hollywood Roosevelt, and you can use an extra bed."

I was grateful to have a place to stay on my arrival back in Los Angeles. The day after I arrived I called Sally Foster. She insisted that I stay with her family. Her sister Polly Ann was married to Carter Herman, a manufacturer, and they had plenty of room for a guest. I felt it was an imposition, and I resisted until Sally remarked, "Oh, by the way, my sister Georgiana will be there tomorrow."

"I will be glad to accept the kind hospitality of your sister and her husband," I said.

That night I could scarcely sleep because of the excitement about finally meeting Georgiana. The moment came in the Hermans' living room the next afternoon. I tried to act nonchalant, and I had my back turned when Georgiana entered the room. I wheeled around to meet her, and my heart fell. She was at least an inch taller than I was!

"Hello, Mr. Montalban."

"Hello, Miss Young."

I could barely stammer out the greeting, so great was my dismay. Then I glanced to the floor and I noticed that she was wearing stylishly high heels. Such relief. I realized that at five feet, eleven inches, I was indeed taller.

There was no time to be wasted. I asked her if I could take her out that night. No, she had a date with a young man who was her steady beau. What about tomorrow night? She had another engagement with the same man. Noticing my crestfallen face, she added, "But maybe I can break it."

I splurged the next night. Cocktails at Romanoff's. Dinner at Thelma Todd's restaurant on the beach at Santa Monica. The best bottle of wine in the house. Dancing at the Trocadero on the Sunset Strip.

Georgiana was everything I had dreamed her to be. At last I had her in my arms on the dance floor at the Trocadero. I gently pressed my cheek to hers, and she did not draw away. I was overwhelmed.

"I love you, Georgiana," I whispered.

To my surprise she replied, "I'm glad."

Driving her home that night, I told her that I could remain in California only three weeks, since I had to return to Mexico

Ricardo Montalban, aged one year, in Mexico City. You can't see it, but there's somebody crouched behind the stone wall holding me up so I don't topple over.

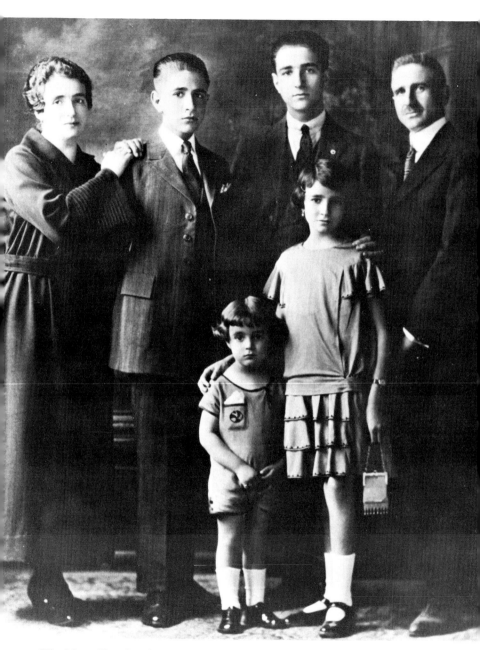

The Montalban family in Mexico City when I was four years old. From left to right: my mother, Ricarda; my brother Pedro; my brother Carlos, who is the famous El Exigente in the Savarin coffee commercials; and my father, Jenaro. The little guy in front is me, protected by my sister, Carmen.

Torreón, Mexico. The family liked the way I looked in my First Communion suit, so a week after the ceremony my mother and I sat for this portrait.

Santa (1942). My first costarring role in Mexican films. The picture was directed by Norman Foster, the husband of Sally Blane; they would later become my brother- and sister-in-law. I played a gypsy bullfighter, and was nominated for a Mexican Academy Award as best supporting actor. I didn't win. (Photo courtesy of Azteca Films, Inc.)

Opposite: this picture of Georgiana was taken when she was a model for Harper's Bazaar. I carried this in my wallet without any of the family knowing it or, for that matter, the real state of my feelings for Georgiana.

A visit to the set of Key to the City *to see my sister-in-law, Loretta Young. We posed for the publicity photographer, and the rest, as they say, is photographic history. (Photo courtesy of Loretta Young.)*

Opposite: this is the tango sequence Cyd Charisse and I did in On an Island with You *for MGM in 1947. I had injured my back, and the choreographer redid the entire dance to favor my right leg, which I could move better than my left leg. (From the MGM release* On an Island with You *© 1948: Loew's Incorporated. Copyright renewed 1975 by Metro-Goldwyn-Mayer, Inc.)*

Latin Lovers (1953), with Lana Turner, my last film under contract to MGM. The studio told me they weren't going to pick up my option, so for the first time in my career, I was on my own as an actor. (From the MGM release Latin Lovers © 1953: Loew's Incorporated.)

and start a movie. "I want to see you every day, every night," I said.

"I think I can arrange that," she replied. And she did, thereby causing her steady to become very angry.

We spent day after day together, and never tired of each other. Each day was a new adventure. We could find pleasure in simple things like a picnic at the beach or visiting the zoo, or simply sitting in the car and pouring out memories of our disparate childhoods. Georgiana's mother was a remarkable woman who managed to keep her family of three daughters and a son together after their father deserted them in Salt Lake City. Mrs. Young brought them to Los Angeles, opened a boardinghouse, and got her children acting jobs in movies at $3.50 a day. Eventually all three daughters became stars—as Polly Ann Young, Sally Blane, and Loretta Young. Mrs. Young married a Los Angeles accountant, George Belzer, and they had one daughter, Georgiana. She was not smitten with the acting life, as were her sisters; she had played only a few roles before *Alexander Graham Bell*, then quit.

Five days remained before I had to return to Mexico City. I didn't want to leave without marrying Georgiana. But there was not enough time. We both were Catholics, and the banns would have to be posted in church for three consecutive Sundays. What could we do? I offered a makeshift plan: we could go to Tijuana for a civil ceremony, then have a church wedding when we returned.

The wedding in Tijuana was as coldly unromantic as could be imagined. A shabby wedding chapel. A pair of witnesses enlisted on the street. But Georgiana and I didn't mind. Legally we were husband and wife. But since we were not married in the eyes of the Church, we both agreed with strong resolve that we would not consummate the marriage. But of course the flesh is weak, and we did.

With great sorrow I took leave of my bride, unhappy that I

could share with no one the news of our marriage—we were determined to keep it secret until the church marriage.

I was now beginning to make important money as a star in Mexico, and I had special need for the salary. I returned for a film, *Fantasia Ranchera*. The shooting went on and on, and I longed for it to finish so I could return to Georgiana. When the schedule finally came to an end, the producers told me they were exercising an option for another film to start immediately.

I was in a quandary. I wanted nothing more than to hurry back to my wife. But I believed that a man should always honor his agreements. Besides, the contract would help buy a home for my bride and myself.

Finally I completed the second movie and rushed back to Georgiana. By this time she was seven months' pregnant.

Georgiana had explained to her family about the Tijuana wedding. All that remained was marriage in the Church, and a quiet ceremony was arranged at St. Paul's in Westwood. Only the family and three other couples gathered in the small chapel. As Georgiana came down the aisle, I was struck once more by how beautiful she was. Something more had been added: the radiance that pregnant women possess.

We both faced the priest, and I helped Georgiana kneel down. I contemplated the solemn beauty of the ancient ritual. I gazed at the altar, then at the priest, then my eyes focused on one of the acolytes, a freckled boy perhaps thirteen. As the priest intoned a prayer, the boy studied Georgiana's face, then looked at her midsection. He gazed again at her face, then his eyes widened as he studied her middle again. Then he turned to look at me.

My eyes snapped shut. I realized I had to concentrate on the ceremony and its significance. And so I prayed, "Please, God, give me guidance for this important step in my life. I realize that I am undertaking a tremendous responsibility. Give me the strength and wisdom to be a good husband and father."

Filled with emotion, I opened my eyes and turned toward Georgiana. She was gone!

Morning sickness had overcome her, and my brother-in-law had hurried forward to assist her out into the fresh air. After several minutes, she returned to the altar, her complexion a light shade of green.

At last we were husband and wife, our union solemnized by the Church. After a brief reception, we drove off to our first home, an apartment in Westwood.

It was a belated honeymoon, but no less a joyous one. We went to the Westwood apartment of Georgiana's mother and talked about the future, whether I should return to Mexico, if she could join me, would the altitude of Mexico City be bad for her pregnancy, etc. The fireplace glowed, the champagne was chilled, everything was in readiness.

Finally, Georgiana decided to go prepare for bed. I finished the champagne, dreaming happily of the immediate future, and then I heard a gasp. And a sob.

"Darling, what is the matter?" I dashed up the stairs to the bedroom. There I found Georgiana, slightly plump but still alluring in her negligee. Weepingly she said, "Look."

I looked. There was no bed in the bedroom, only a mattress lying on the floor. Georgiana's mother, a brilliant decorator with the forgetfulness of an artist, had somehow ordered the bedstead transferred to another apartment. We were left with only a mattress.

"Don't fret, Georgiana," I said, holding her in my arms, "our married life can only improve after this."

"This is a work weekend," said Father O'Gara at our four-fifteen afternoon conference in the chapel. The theme of work has appeared over and over again. We are told that we must work in order to make the retreat successful.

On a retreat, work means prayer, and we retreatants

were given much good advice on how to pray. Also how not to pray. Father O'Gara told us about the Irish woman who made her entreaty: "God, you can't say you can't and you won't say you won't, so you will, won't you?"

Father O'Gara pointed out the difficulty in concentrating on prayer, and he told the story of St. Alphonse. He was conversing with a man who professed to be godly and bragged about his ability to pray. St. Alphonse challenged him: "I will give you my horse if you can think only of God for thirty minutes." The man replied, "Of course I can!" and he knelt in devout prayer. After fifteen minutes he looked up at St. Alphonse and asked, "The saddle, too?"

As a guide to our praying, we were given two pages of suggestions by Father Armand Nigro, S.J.

"GOD SPEAKS TO US FIRST: This fundamental truth makes it possible for us to pray to God. He has been concerned for each of us long before we became concerned for ourselves. He desires communication with us. . . .

"HE INVITES US TO LISTEN: Our response to God's initial move is to *listen* to what He is saying. This is the basic attitude of prayer. . . ."

Father Nigro offers five *P*'s as a guide to preparing for prayer:

1. Pick a passage from Scripture. Have it marked and ready.

2. Place—where you are alone and uninhibited in your response to God's presence.

3. Posture—relaxed and peaceful. A harmony with body and spirit.

4. Presence of God. Be aware of it and acknowledge and respond to it. If nothing happens, or if you are hungry to hear God's word, then . . .

5. Pray the passage from Scripture. Read it very slowly aloud and listen carefully and peacefully to it.

Father Basset joined us at dinner, and with his precise English logic he offered further advice on prayer. We should follow the advice of Jesus, who said, "When you pray, go into your inner room and shut the door on yourself, and then your Father, who sees in secret, will reward you."

The greatest crisis in a retreat, said Father Basset, "is when I'm alone in my room and nobody's looking, how do I pray?" It is not easy, he admitted, because most of us are unaccustomed to solitude. He told of once giving the last rites to a man who was watching television; the man was dying, but he wouldn't give up watching some inane show.

"St. Augustine pointed out how seldom any of us laughs in private," Father Basset remarked.

How true. How little time I have had for private mirth or solitary thought during the past few frantic years. And how soul-refreshing it is to savor the hours of quietude.

Dinner again was hearty: roast beef, mashed potatoes and gravy, zucchini, green salad, French rolls, chocolate pudding. And again the delight of a fine French wine. After the meal Father O'Mara talked about the Blessed Mother at the shrine to Mary behind the main house. Then we retreatants had a quiet contemplative hour at twilight. Some sat on the veranda, smoking cigarettes and listening to the calls of the night birds. Others strolled among the groves of trees, smiling without speaking as they passed each other.

I found a place where I could be alone to think about my faith and how it has developed since my childhood. I am a Catholic because my parents were

Catholics; it's as simple as that. And still, it's not simple at all. The faith that I feel now is far different from what I knew as a child, and I arrived at it through a long and sometimes difficult search.

The nuns were my earliest teachers. In grammar school they were stern disciplinarians, yet with an underlying sweetness. I viewed them with both awe and affection, impressed that they would totally dedicate their lives to the Church.

Father Fajanel was another inspiration in my life. He was a French priest who defied the Mexican government's edict that religion could not be taught to children. For three years I attended clandestine classes he taught in the attic of a home. The students were arranged in five rows, each a different grade. How Father Fajanel managed to teach five different classes, I can't tell you. But he did. He was an inspiration, a man so dedicated to his religious beliefs that he would risk imprisonment to instruct children.

I received my First Communion in the basement of a convent. I was with five other Torreón youngsters in a ceremony that was held by candlelight for fear the police might detect us. It is hard to imagine such a thing happening in Mexico, but the government was determined to stamp out the influence of the Church. The suppression did not succeed. When the edict was lifted, the faith of the people was stronger than ever. Always under stress the muscle is tightened.

The government ban on religious instruction prevailed during my year with the Maristas priests in Mexico City. But there could be no mistaking the faith that underlay their teaching. I learned from them a sense of discipline, a different kind from what I had learned at home in Torreón. The students were treated as men, not as children. We were expected to respond to the logic of discipline, not simply do what we were told to do.

The religion of my youth was emotional, varying according

to my mood. When I was sad, I prayed, "Dear God, please help me." When I was frustrated, I blamed God for my troubles. Communion had a profound effect on me. I became so suffused with emotion that tears came to my eyes.

When I became a young man, my religion remained on the grammar school level. It might easily have fallen under the impact of a sophisticated world.

The first to question my faith was Seki Sano. As a Communist, he was naturally anti-Church, and he argued that the Catholic hierarchy collaborated in the oppression of the peons. I listened to his anti-religion arguments unconvinced, and yet my faith was questioned.

When I came to the United States, I lived and worked among a great many non-Catholics, and many of them were critical of the Church. I was asked questions about my faith, and often I was unable to supply answers. I felt perplexed and frustrated.

Through my agent, Manning O'Connor, I became acquainted with Father Walsh Murray, a priest who taught at Loyola University. He was a big, vital, outgoing Irishman with a broad background in theology and a passionate interest in sports. In recent years he has become chaplain of the San Diego Chargers pro football team. Manning O'Connor, Father Murray, and I often went together to football games and boxing matches, all three of us being rabid fans.

Father Murray never mentioned religious matters, but I think he must have sensed my questioning attitude. There were certain perplexities that remained unanswered in my mind. I'm not a believer in blind faith. I think it is your duty to ask questions about matters that puzzle you. Unanswered questions begin to pry and weaken your beliefs. Religion is bolstered by being challenged.

One day I expressed my feelings to Father Murray.

"When I was a boy, going to Communion gave me a sensation of peace and beauty," I told him. "It was a very solemn moment in my life. It filled me with overwhelming emotion. Serenity would invade my spirit.

"When I became an actor in Mexico, I went to church every Sunday, but I didn't receive Communion as often as I had as a child. When I did receive Communion, it still had a tremendous impact on me, a feeling of rejoicing and beauty.

"Then I came to this country, and my wife was a Catholic. I don't say a 'good' Catholic or a 'practicing' Catholic, because I think you either are one or you're not. So she was a Catholic. We went to Church, of course, and I began receiving Communion more often. In fact, every Sunday. But then Communion became a familiar activity, so much so that I felt absolutely no emotion. I tried to concentrate more on what was happening to me. I was receiving the body and the blood of Jesus Christ, my Lord. What a magnificent and wonderful moment that is. And yet it didn't move me."

Father Murray smiled and said, "Congratulations. *Now* you are a Catholic. Before, you were an emotional man. A selfish man, who wanted to derive from Communion great joy. Now you are doing it out of intellectual conviction. Intellectual conviction is constant; emotion is not. I'm sure that when things were going well for you, you took your religion for granted. When you had troubled times, you went to church and prayed. Am I right?"

"Absolutely, Father."

"Emotion. Your faith had its highs and its lows. But now you are a constant Catholic. You don't have those soaring moments. But you're not subjected to the lapses, either."

Father Murray helped me in many ways. He cited philosophers for me to read. We had long talks about a myriad of matters, including freedom.

"Freedom is the right to do what you *ought* to do," he explained. "Notice I don't say what you *must* do, which is oppression. Nor do I say what you *want* to do, which is chaos.

"If you come upon a park bench marked 'wet paint,' you

have the freedom to sit down. But if you did, you would get your suit ruined. Supposing you drive to a stop signal. You bring your car to a halt, let the other cars cross, then proceed yourself. If the stop sign were not there, you would face a traffic jam."

Still, the concept of freedom was not clear to me. I discussed it once with Richard Burton, who gave me a definition that is used in England: "Freedom is a spirited horse with an easy halter."

That made sense, but I didn't really grasp the essence of freedom until I went to Japan for *Sayonara*. It was a challenge for a Mexican actor to portray a Japanese Kabuki player, and I wanted to have the best possible preparation. That meant going to Japan two months before the film was to start shooting. It meant being away from my family at Christmas, but the opportunity was important to my career.

Hour after hour, day after day, I worked with a Kabuki master, Masaya Fujima.

"No, the index finger must be a little more curved," Fujima corrected me, "and it must be parallel with the little finger. The thumb should touch the first joint of the little finger. . . ."

That was only for the position of the hands. Then I had to learn the position of my eyes and head in relation to the lion's head I was holding in my other hand. As I started to move, all the positions changed, and I had to learn another stance. The movements had to be precise, the body swaying to one side, then the other.

One night I went back to my hotel, slumped in a chair, and wept bitter tears of frustration. It was all too foreign to me; I would never learn it. I would look like a fool to the Japanese, like an idiot to the Americans. What the hell was so important about getting your finger curved just so?

But I knew why it was so important. The Kabuki was the most traditional theater in the world, and you had to do it the right way. I returned the following day for another grueling session.

Then one day it came to me. The Kabuki movements became my movements. As an actor I experienced a freedom that I had never known before, nor have I since. I realized that only through discipline can you achieve freedom. Pour water in a cup and you can drink from it. Without a cup the water would splash all over. The cup is discipline.

"Time doesn't exist," Father Murray told me. "With our finite minds we try to explain the phenomenon of change, and we call it time. But if you were traveling at an enormous speed through space, you would not age the same as you do on earth. So time is relative."

When that concept seemed difficult for me to grasp, he offered an example:

"Supposing you are standing on a bridge over a stream of rushing water. You drop a rock into the current and you say, 'Now!' By the time you get out the first sound of the word, the moment has passed. So there is no such thing as now. Time does not exist. The important thing is that I AM, and therefore I must be good. Not that I was good yesterday, or I will be good tomorrow. The past and the future do not exist. *Now* does not even exist. All that exists is I AM."

Again, Japan helped me understand this difficult concept.

When I attended the Kabuki theater, I was surprised by the reaction of the audience. The people would not necessarily applaud at the end of the play. But during the performance the reaction could be spontaneous and effusive. A movement or a song by an actor could evoke cheers from a segment of the audience and shouts of the actor's name.

The *moment* was important to the Japanese, not the cumulative effect of the performance. The past doesn't exist because it has ceased to be; the future doesn't exist because it hasn't happened. They believe in the present moment.

I understood that when I went to a restaurant with my interpreter and his friends. We could sit in silence and no one felt embarrassed. We didn't need to invent idle talk if we had nothing to say. We simply enjoyed each other's presence at that moment. We could contemplate the beauty of a painted screen or the symmetry of a gravel garden outside the window. Or simply listen to the sound of a small fountain or the tinkling of a tiny bell in the wind. The kimonoed waitress served the food with dainty elegance, and the food itself was artistically prepared. We savored the sake and then admired the cup it was served in, handcrafted and painted by an artist.

This attitude of making the most of the moment has colored my whole life. I respect the past, but I do not live in it. I used to keep scripts and photographs as mementos of all the movies I have been in. Now I save nothing. The future holds no concern for me. What comes will come.

The *moment* is everything.

As a boy and even as a young man, I used to pray to God for specific things: "Dear God, make my mother well again. . . ." "Bring Georgiana safely through this childbirth, Lord. . . ." "Heavenly Father, I beseech you . . ."

Often my prayers were answered, sometimes not. I continued to direct my pleas to the Creator. Then one night in St. Malachy's Church in Manhattan, a simple incident changed my entire attitude toward prayer.

It was in 1959, and I was appearing on Broadway in the second year of *Jamaica*, a musical in which I costarred with Lena Horne. I liked the show, and Lena was a joy to work with, but I was miserable. Two years is a long time to be performing the same role night after night, especially when you're separated from your family.

Georgiana and the children had been with me at the beginning of the run. But I didn't know how long *Jamaica* would last, and so Georgiana took the children home so their school

terms would not be interrupted. And *Jamaica* went on and on.
I reached the point where I hadn't seen my family in four
months.

My dresser was a marvelous man named Charlie Blackstone.
He was black, and a warm, gracious person; we became excellent friends during the long run. Every Saturday night we made
a custom of attending Midnight Mass at St. Malachy's, the actors' church—Charlie was also a Catholic.

I was weary after a matinee and an evening performance, and
I faced another Sunday without my family. I guess I didn't realize how lonely I was, because I made a stupid prayer: "Dear
God, don't keep this play running so long. I've had it. If I
don't get back to my family I'm going to have a nervous break-
down. I want to go home."

Opening my eyes, I glanced over to Charlie, who was also
kneeling in prayer. I realized instantly what his prayer was:
"Thank you, God, for this play. It's not easy to get jobs nowadays, and I'm grateful for this long run. I hope it runs forever."

From that time on, I have never prayed for selfish things. My
prayer is always this:

"Thy will be done, on earth as it is in heaven."

After night prayers, we retreatants again had time
alone. The Azusa foothills offered a comforting still-
ness that was conducive to taking stock, both personally and professionally. I'm sure that my fellow retreatants gave thought to their aspirations as judges,
doctors, farmers, mechanics, teachers, salesmen, and
students. And naturally I thought of my career as
actor.

"Fantasy Island" is important to me. Any project
that I undertake is the most important thing in my
professional life, whether it is a thirty-second commercial, a guest role in a television movie, a play in a
theater-in-the-round, or an appearance at a Mexican-

American fiesta. To each I devote my total attention and special care.

Since I am an integral part of "Fantasy Island," it is an integral part of me. I always bring to it my enthusiasm, my total preparation, my professionalism. Movie and stage actors sometimes scoff, "It's only television, Ricardo." I don't see it that way. To me it is a dignified way of presenting entertainment to the people—within the limitations of budget, time, and mass media.

Actors are the most insecure people in the world. For thirty-five years I have had a roller-coaster career, with the down periods outweighing those on top. Hence I saw in "Fantasy Island" the chance for a wonderful ribbon to tie onto my career as a working actor. It could provide the security I had always sought but could never achieve. It could also mean that my wife would always be secure and would not become a burden to our children or the government.

Mr. Roarke was not an easy role to approach. When I first read the script, I said, "Who is this man? Is he a magician? A hypnotist? Does he use hallucinogenic drugs?" I finally came across a character that worked for me. This man is capable of all those things. He has the essence of mystery, but I needed to have a point of view so my performance would be consistent. I decided to play him 95 percent believable and 5 percent mystery. He doesn't have to behave mysteriously; only what he does is mysterious.

Once I had decided on this attitude, I felt comfortable with Mr. Roarke. Then followed the agonizing months as the ABC network tried different formats to present to the television audience. The first show was a two-hour movie. Then we did a two-part story of an hour apiece. Then four single hours. All this was designed to find out whether the audience would accept the rather daring premise of an island resort where people could actually live out their fantasies.

During all this time I did not dare place too much hope that "Fantasy Island" would succeed. The critics helped to curb my expectations. Their reviews were not just bad; they were abysmal.

After I had done the tryout segments, my friend Earl Holliman asked me to appear in a play at a Texas theater of which he was part owner. I told him I was interested. Not only did I enjoy the theater; it was necessary to occupy the slack in my movie and television career.

"Could you wait for an answer until I can read the reviews on 'Fantasy Island' next Monday?" I asked Earl.

"Are you worried about reviews?" he asked.

"Of course."

"Don't, Ricardo. Have you any idea what the critics said about 'Police Woman'? Or 'All in the Family,' or 'Laverne and Shirley,' or 'Love Boat'? They all got rotten reviews, and they lasted."

That gave me hope, but I still wasn't prepared for the lambasting of "Fantasy Island." My heart sank. I had known the power of critics in the theater, where a handful of demigods wielded power of life and death over the future of actors. Movie reviewers did not possess such absolute power, but their opinions could help or hurt a project.

Thank heaven I was in a medium in which the public decided whether or not they liked a show. They liked "Fantasy Island." The series had been on the air only a few times when suddenly I was recognized everywhere I went, by all age groups.

I had never known such widespread recognition.

During my early years at MGM, I drew attention
from the bobby-soxers. Later, when I was appearing in
the theater and television movies, I was recognized by
a mature segment of the public. Since "Fantasy Island," it happens with all ages. One day on my way
home from the studio, I was waiting at a signal when
a group of seven-year-olds skimmed by on skateboards.
One of them shouted, "Hey, there's Ricardo Montalban!"

"Fantasy Island" has required certain adjustments
in my life. I don't get to see my wife. I rise at five,
leave the house at six, and I'm seldom home until
eight or nine in the evening. But that's the way a television series is, and I can't complain. I tell myself,
"This is what I want to do: to act."

I had to make another adjustment at the studio.
The entire production team of "Fantasy Island" became another family, with many diverse personalities.
The star of the show feels a certain responsibility to
help maintain a happy but disciplined set. The greater
the privilege, the greater the responsibility. So I carry
on my shoulders the responsibility of setting the tone
so there will be no tension. Talented people cannot
do their best work when they are tense.

I always arrive ten or fifteen minutes before my call.
I am always prepared for my day's work. I try to maintain a happy countenance and a rapport with the
crew, cast, and guest stars.

An actor asked me, "How do you get along with
Hervé?" That is one of the blessings of "Fantasy Island": I have great fondness for Hervé. I respect him,
I admire him, and I look forward each time I work
with him.

"Boy, are you lucky!" said my actor friend. "I did a

series with an actor I couldn't stand. I had to swallow hard every time I did a scene with him."

I can't think of anything worse. I am blessed with a costar who is extremely talented and intelligent, and possessed of a marvelous sense of humor. Hervé can laugh at himself, which is remarkable when you consider the life that he has led. It is not easy to live in a world where everyone is twice as tall as you are. At one time when he was young, he didn't even want to go out of his house. In public he has taken abuse—it's surprising there are so many sick people in the world. Hervé has also had to endure physical pain. Because of his structure, he has difficulty getting in and out of cars, of bending. At times when the weather is damp and we have been standing a long time, both of us are in considerable pain, and we compare notes.

Hervé and I have arrived at an understanding that is essential for costars. Because I have had more experience in acting, I sometimes say, "Now, Hervé, I have a suggestion that might help this scene play better." Often he will say, "Hey, that's a good idea!" Once in a while, he says, "No, I think it's better this way." He is secure enough to accept or reject a suggestion; he never resents one.

Our relationship must be permeated by love. I feel that for him, and I have reason to believe that he feels the same toward me. It is essential that Roarke and Tattoo have affection for each other, and so it is convenient that Montalban and Villechaize also do. I have always felt that the relationship between Roarke and Tattoo should be the same as that between Stan Laurel and Oliver Hardy. They could push each other or throw pies in each other's face or cut off ties, and we never resented that. Because we knew they loved each other.

One of my close friends provided another comparison: "The relationship between Roarke and Tattoo is the same as the one between Edgar Bergen and Charlie McCarthy. It has nothing to do with size. Charlie was the feisty little guy who was always ogling the girls. Edgar was the boss who treated Charlie gently, but at a given moment Charlie could be put away in his box. Still, you always had the sense that Edgar and Charlie loved each other."

In 1945 my life was changing in swift, dramatic ways. Not only had I become a husband and father, my acting career was also destined for a complete change.

I had every intention of continuing my career as an actor in Mexican films. With my accent and my obviously Latin background, I could see no place for me in Hollywood movies, which were then specializing in all-American-boy types like Van Johnson and Sonny Tufts.

Besides, I was happy in Mexican movies. I was being recognized because of the success of my films, and with the recognition came financial reward. I could earn $20,000 per picture and make five a year. Taxes were negligible, so I was able to live well and save money, too.

The atmosphere in the Mexican film industry was extremely pleasant. There was no caste system, such as I was to discover in Hollywood. Cantinflas was the biggest star, but he was friendly with everyone, from producers to prop boys. It was the same with everyone else. We all had a spirit of camaraderie, perhaps because Mexicans are not inclined to take certain things too seriously. No star could ever put on airs; he would have been kidded to death.

During my four years in Mexican films I had made many good friends, and I felt I was maturing as an actor. Partly it was because of the teaching of Seki Sano, partly because I was given opportunities in films to stretch my dramatic muscles.

Mexican movies were flourishing during the mid-1940s. New directors, writers, and actors were emerging, and they had the freedom to attempt serious films. The cost of making movies was reasonable, hence producers could afford to take chances on subjects that might not be considered surefire box office.

After the church wedding, I had to return to Mexico for another film. Naturally, I had wanted to bring Georgiana along so we could settle in our own home in Mexico City. But because her pregnancy had been difficult, the doctor believed the air trip and the altitude of Mexico City might be risky for her. Sadly I returned to Mexico alone.

At the same time, a producer from Metro-Goldwyn-Mayer, Jack Cummings, was in Mexico searching for locations for a film to star Esther Williams, *Fiesta.* He was also looking for an actor who could portray Esther's twin brother, a bullfighter. One day Cummings happened to be in the same restaurant where I was lunching. He glanced at me and commented to his companion, "Now that's the kind of face I'm looking for."

Later Cummings went to a studio to meet a friend from Hollywood, Norman Foster. Norman had just directed me in *La Hora de la Verdad,* a bullfighting picture, and he screened it for his visitor.

"That's the guy!" the producer exclaimed. "He's the one I saw in the restaurant!"

"He's my brother-in-law," Norman replied.

I was totally unaware of these goings-on. I was hurrying to finish a film, *Pepita Jiménez,* so I could race back to Los Angeles for the birth of my first child.

My arrival came only two days before Georgiana started having labor pains. I rushed her to St. Vincent's Hospital near downtown Los Angeles, arriving at noon. The pains subsided, then began again at two. I stayed with her until late afternoon, when she started getting drowsy. I went to the waiting room.

Thoughts raced through my head. Supposing something happened to Georgiana. How could I live without her? How could

I live with the guilt of having caused her suffering? I hated to see her in pain. I hated the torture of waiting, waiting.

Among the other fathers in the room was a man who remained totally nonchalant. He detected my nervousness and said, "It's simply routine. I been through this thing six times; this is my seventh. Relax." He continued reading the newspaper and smoking his cigar.

Relax? Impossible! My nerves frayed further as the nurse began making announcements.

"Mr. Jones, you have a baby girl, six and a half pounds."

Mr. Jones left happily, and the veteran father didn't even look up from his paper.

"Mr. Ramirez, it's a girl; seven pounds, eight ounces."

"Not bad," said the veteran. The routine continued through the evening, and all of the fathers had girls. At 1 A.M., the nurse announced a girl for the man with the cigar. He shrugged and left the room.

Waiting, waiting. Finally, at 3 A.M., the nurse came to the door.

"Mr. Montalban?"

"YES."

"Congratulations. A baby girl; nine pounds, two ounces."

"Isn't that wonderful!" I glanced around to share my joy and realized I was the only father left in the waiting room.

I went to the nursery, and the nurse held up the newborn infant. A beautiful round head, rosy cheeks. She looked like a tiny, lovely girl, not the red-faced baby I had expected. Georgiana was resting. She had been through tremendous pain, and I felt so sorry for her. As I watched her sleeping quietly on the hospital bed, my love for her was stronger than I ever felt it could be.

"Is this Ricardo Montalban?" The voice on the telephone sounded tough and Irish.

"Yes."

"This is Manning O'Connor." I recognized the name, having met him and his wife, Peggy. "I'm an agent, you know. I handle Jeanne Crain, Rod Cameron, a few others. You got an agent?"

"No. I don't work in Hollywood."

"You might."

"I don't think so, Mr. O'Connor. In fact, I'm making plans to move my wife and my new daughter to Mexico City."

"Hold off. A friend of mine happens to be Eddie Mannix."

"Who's Eddie Mannix?"

"Boy, you don't know Hollywood, do you? Eddie Mannix is a big shot at MGM, one of the most powerful men in the industry."

"And?"

"And the studio wants to test you for a part in an Esther Williams movie. If they like you, you'll get a contract out of it."

It was an exciting prospect. Imagine being signed at MGM, the biggest studio in Hollywood, with the biggest roster of stars. But would I get lost in such a stellar array? Would they be able to cast an actor with a decided accent? I was already well established in Mexican films; I could probably have a long and successful career in Mexico. Should I throw all that away in the chancy pursuit of a Hollywood career? I realized how the American movie business could discard its favorites as swiftly as they had been created.

I discussed the future with Georgiana. We agreed I should try for the MGM contract. Yes, the Mexican career was as safe and secure as any actor's life could be. But Hollywood was a far greater arena, a place from which I could reach audiences of the world, not merely those who spoke Spanish.

Robert Z. Leonard, who had made *The Great Ziegfeld*, *Dancing Lady*, and *Maytime*, directed my first test. I played a scene from *Gaslight*, acting the Charles Boyer role with a contract actress, Jacqueline White, playing the Ingrid Bergman part. I must have performed adequately because the studio ordered another test, this time a scene from *Fiesta*. I was given a seven-year contract, with options. Beginning salary was $1,250 a week, forty weeks a year; twelve weeks' layoff.

I toured the MGM studio as wide-eyed as any tourist. On Lot 3, I found the jungle where Johnny Weissmuller ruled as Tarzan, the street where Judy Garland pined for "the boy next door" in *Meet Me in St. Louis*. On Lot 2, I visited the Hardy Family's house and the village where Mrs. Miniver had lived. Every one of the thirty stages was occupied by movies that were shooting or sets that were being built. The streets were filled at lunchtime with actors and extras in all kinds of costumes. It was like attending a huge masquerade party.

The commissary was a dazzling sight. Clark Gable and Spencer Tracy sitting together at the actors' table, Robert Taylor nearby. Katharine Hepburn all alone in a corner. Lewis Stone, Ethel and Lionel Barrymore, Jane Powell, Fred Astaire, Jimmy Durante, June Allyson, Frank Sinatra, Red Skelton, Kathryn Grayson, Gene Kelly, Ava Gardner, Judy Garland, many more. Some of them even said hello to me as we passed on the studio streets.

Fiesta was an easy film for me in one respect: much of it was shot in Mexico. But it was difficult in another way. I had to dance.

It made no difference that I had done little dancing besides a fox-trot at the senior prom at Fairfax High. I was assigned to perform a number under the direction of Eugene Loring. My partner: Cyd Charisse.

I must say that Cyd, who is one of the most gifted and exquisite dancers in the world, was extremely patient with me. So was Gene Loring. Perhaps they recognized my eagerness to succeed. I spent long hours in the rehearsal hall, trying to coax my body into responding to the music. It was no easy task to perform with a totally professional partner when you yourself had no previous training whatsoever. But I was determined to learn.

I realized that the more versatile a performer I proved myself, the more valuable I would be to MGM.

Esther Williams, my twin sister in *Fiesta*, proved to be easy to work with. She had a warm, outgoing personality with an ability to laugh at herself and life in general. She had just married Ben Gage, and they spent their honeymoon on the Mexican location. Richard Thorpe's direction was helpful, but I felt inadequate in the impressive cast, which included John Carroll, Mary Astor, Akim Tamiroff, Hugo Haas, Fortunio Bonanova, and Frank Puglia. I suffered through the rushes. I worried about wrinkling my forehead or making the wrong gesture, and as a result I was terribly self-conscious on the next day of shooting. It was a mistake, fretting over details when I should have applied myself to the overall characterization. After *Fiesta* I vowed never to attend rushes again.

Fiesta proved to be a good showcase for me. The reviews declared that I was a promising new performer, and my stock rose at MGM. Jack Cummings escorted me to the executive dining room, and there I met the powers at the studio—Benny Thau, Eddie Mannix, L. K. Sidney, Mervyn Leroy, Joe Pasternak, Arthur Freed, Pandro Berman, and others. Then one day Cummings took me to Louis B. Mayer's private dining room, just off the main commissary. "Young man, I think you've got great promise," Mr. Mayer said to me. I walked out of the room on a cloud.

On an Island with You came next, again with Esther, as well as Cyd Charisse, Peter Lawford, Jimmy Durante, Leon Ames, Dick Simmons, and Xavier Cugat's orchestra. When *The Kissing Bandit* seemed to be a loser for Frank Sinatra and Kathryn Grayson, Joe Pasternak added a dance sequence with Cyd, Ann Miller, and myself. It was called "The Dance of Fury." It was furious, all right, but not enough to save the picture.

Next came *Neptune's Daughter*, once more with Esther Williams. This time I not only danced, I sang. One number was a delight: Frank Loesser's "Baby, It's Cold Outside," which won an Academy Award as best song of 1949. My other song was "My Heart Beats Faster," which won nothing.

I recorded "My Heart Beats Faster," with Georgie Stoll conducting a huge orchestra on the music stage. A week later he told me, "Look, Ricardo, you were nervous; let's try it again with just a microphone and the orchestra track on earphones." A week later Georgie said, "Ricardo, I'm sure you were under pressure with the engineer staring at you; let's record it again on an empty stage." So we went to a stage and we talked a bit to loosen me up, then I faced a microphone with only Georgie watching. When he heard the playback, he said, "Maybe it will sound better if you sit on a stool." Next, "Let's try it with you lying down on a couch." He finally ended up using the first recording.

I'm not a singer (though I have learned to sell a song through the lyric). I'm not a dancer. Yet my first four movies at MGM turned out to be musicals. This despite the fact that everything I had done in Mexico was highly dramatic. I couldn't understand why the studio was trying to make me into something that I really wasn't. But there was no arguing with the producers. They had complete control of your destiny.

After Dore Schary became head of production in 1948, more emphasis was placed on drama, and at last I had a chance to show that I could do something else besides dance. Schary cast me as a Mexican American from East Los Angeles in his personal production, *Battleground*. I did *Border Incident* with John Sturges and *Mystery Street* with Anthony Mann as director. Both movies got wonderful reviews and even some awards, but they were B pictures and didn't draw much attention. I had another good role as a prizefighter in *Right Cross*, with Dick Powell and June Allyson, also Marilyn Monroe in a bit role. But then it was back to musicals with *Two Weeks with Love*, costarring with Jane Powell.

I never did get the big dramatic role that is so important for an actor's career. I never have gotten it in Hollywood. I have accepted that. I have tried to pursue my acting craft to the best of my ability, and those years at MGM were invaluable.

I had to learn new techniques with the move from Mexico City to Hollywood. Strangely enough, I felt more comfortable speaking English in films than I had with Spanish. Americans speak succinctly, using common words to get the meaning across. Spanish-speaking people pride themselves in their vocabularies. They try not to repeat the same words when they speak, and in writing the process is carried one step farther: the language becomes extremely flowery. And so the scriptwriters in Mexico ladened their scenarios with words. The dialogue seemed unnatural to me, and I struggled to make the stilted dialogue sound like everyday talk.

That problem didn't exist in Hollywood. Screenwriters had keen ears for natural conversation; their dialogue was crisp and to the point. It was easy for me to speak, though I had to curb the tendency of all Latin actors to overstate. I toned myself down, learned how to play in concert with the other actors.

My best teacher was Spencer Tracy. I made a habit of finding out when he was working, and I sneaked onto his sets and watched him from behind scenery. Sometimes I couldn't see him, but I could hear his voice delivering the lines in a perfectly natural way.

Another teacher was Louis Calhern. We did a couple of pictures together, and I cherished his advice. Once he told me, "When you're playing a character and you want the audience to like you, you must never hate the antagonist. You must hate what the antagonist *does*. Don't hate the villain, let the audience hate him; they will hate him more. But—if you want to be disliked by the audience, then dislike the other character."

It was sound advice, and it coincided with my Catholic teaching: Hate the sin, but love the sinner.

My acting career almost came to an end one cloudless day in Colorado in 1950. I had ridden my horse to the crest of a hill,

Sayonara (1957). I played Nakamura-san, a Kabuki actor. The film was the story of three interracial couples (Patricia Owens and I were one, Marlon Brando and Miiko Taka and Red Buttons and Miyoshi Umeki were the starring couples). I was and still am very pleased with my performance and very much saddened by this picture. I was hoping for an Academy Award nomination, but unfortunately, most of my scenes ended up on the cutting room floor. (Photo courtesy of Warner Bros., Inc.)

Sweet Charity (1969), with Shirley MacLaine. I played a suave, elegant actor to Shirley's dance hall girl. In this scene I lead her, suavely and elegantly, onto the dance floor and she proceeds, as you can guess from my reaction, to implant her stiletto heel on my toe. (From the motion picture Sweet Charity. Courtesy of Universal Pictures.)

Something different yet again. Learning and rehearsing the massive role of Don Juan for the touring company of Shaw's Don Juan in Hell (1972). The other members of the troupe were Agnes Moorehead, Edward Mulhare, and Paul Henreid. John Houseman of "Paper Chase" fame was our director. (Photo courtesy of Lee Orgel, producer, Don Juan in Hell, B.&T. Co.)

How the West Was Won (1978), *with James Arness. I played the role of the Indian chief Santangkai, of the Sioux nation. From the moment I read the part I sensed something special about it. And I was right! (From the MGM television release "How the West Was Won"* © 1977: Metro-Goldwyn-Mayer, Inc.)

The night of the Emmy Awards, September 17, 1978. For my performance as Chief Santangkai, I won an Emmy for Best Supporting Actor in a Dramatic Series. Here I am sharing the big moment with the winner for Best Supporting Actress, Blanche Baker, who was honored for her role in Holocaust. (United Press International Photo.)

One of the happiest moments nowadays is a quiet moment with Georgiana at home.

With Hervé Villechaize. If I have ever been happy as an actor, it is now as I work with Hervé on "Fantasy Island." I feel extremely fortunate that, after so many years of struggling, I am doing a series that has proved successful with an actor for whom I have sincere respect and affection. (Photo courtesy of Columbia Pictures Television, a division of Columbia Pictures Industries, Inc.)

Mr. Roarke of "Fantasy Island." This photo is a publicity still for the original two-hour television movie. As originally envisioned, Mr. Roarke was a complete man of mystery, and the audience at first didn't know if he was a good or bad man. However, as the series progresses, Mr. Roarke is definitely not a villain, although still most enigmatic. (Photo courtesy of Columbia Pictures Television, a division of Columbia Pictures Industries, Inc.)

and I gazed all around me. In the distance I could see the ma-
jestic Colorado peaks, still whitened despite the summer sun.
The valley was rimmed with smaller mountains, green with
tall, straight-standing pines. On the grassy meadow below me I
saw the dwarfed figures of men and horses. The film company
was preparing for a battle scene.

I felt good. The rare, crisp air seemed to give my body added
strength, and that would be useful in the weeks ahead. My role
in *Across the Wide Missouri* would be strenuous. It was also
one of the best I had ever been given at MGM. William Wellman was directing, and I had developed a good relationship
with him in *Battleground*. It was an excellent cast, including
Maria Elena Marques, with whom I had worked in my first
film in Mexico, as well as Adolphe Menjou, John Hodiak, J.
Carroll Naish, Jack Holt, Alan Napier, Richard Anderson, and
Douglas Fowley. The star: Clark Gable.

This was my first movie with The King. I had known him
slightly at the studio, only in passing. On a film location you really get acquainted with your fellow actors, and I admit I was
disappointed with Clark Gable. Not that I found him lacking
as a man. He simply didn't fulfill my image of him as a super
superstar. I expected him to be Rhett Butler, but he wasn't at
all. He was completely down-to-earth, easy to talk to, and totally professional. Always he was the first actor on the set, and
he never had to ask the script girl, "What's the line here?" He
knew his dialogue and he did his work with no wasted energy.
He didn't theorize about acting; it was just a job to him. He
much preferred to talk about hunting, fishing, and automobiles.

I had prepared for my role. I was playing a Blackfoot warrior,
and I studied the tribe's language and customs with an authority, Nippo Strongheart. I exercised and rode horseback so I
could convincingly portray an Indian brave. I arrived early at
the location near Durango and watched the filming, swam in
the motel pool, and enjoyed the brisk, clean atmosphere of the
Rockies. As I stood on the hill overlooking the location, I de-

cided it was time to get acquainted with the horse I was to ride in the movie. Two days later my role would begin, and I wanted to be sure that the horse and I would be comfortable together.

He was a magnificent animal, a pinto that pranced around the corral full of raw energy. The Colorado air seemed to have envigorated him, too; also the fresh mountain grass. The pinto had been shipped from Los Angeles, and hadn't been ridden in a couple of weeks; he was feeling bright and frisky.

I had to ride him Indian-style in the movie, and I decided to give it a tryout. No saddle. Not even a halter, only a piece of rope tied around his jaw. I liked the idea of giving horse and rider an authentic, exciting, primitive look. But first I'd better see if I could control the pinto with only a piece of rope. I catapulted onto his back.

The pinto responded immediately, instinctively, reacting as if he had never had a rider on his back. Not leaping like a bronco, but prancing with total independence. "Time to let him know who's the boss, Ricardo," I instructed myself.

I tightened the rein. I realized I would have to establish my control or he would never perform before the camera. At first I tried to walk him. Impossible. He was simply not inclined to walk. I tried a gentle gallop, but it didn't work.

"Okay, pardner, if you want to run, we'll run," I said, and I opened him up. The pinto went racing across the hill, and I felt the exhilaration of a roller coaster at an amusement park. But unlike in a roller coaster, I felt in control. I held tightly to the rein, and I let him know who was boss. I guided him down the hill and then turned him gently around, so he had to climb the incline. This would tire him, I realized, and bring him under better control. Now he was beginning to gentle, to realize the fatigue that came with exertion in the mile-high atmosphere. He slowed, and I let him walk. Then I urged a gallop, and walked him again. He became more responsive. Now he welcomed the chance to abandon the chase.

I rode him to the top of the hill, where sprouts of grass were pushing through the earth. He seemed exhausted, and I welcomed the chance to rest myself. I turned sideways on the horse, loosening the rope so he could graze. With my left leg dangling, I gazed idly down at the film company in the meadow.

BOOM!

All of a sudden a prop cannon on the film location below exploded with a noise that ricocheted off the mountain walls. I was startled, the pinto was terrified. He started racing down the hill. He was not bucking, but he kicked up his legs as he raced along, and it was impossible for me to regain a riding position. All I could do was hold on as well as possible and hope that the frightened horse would run out of steam.

But he didn't. He kept hurtling down the slope faster and faster, and the ride was getting bouncier. I was not frightened, because I had been thrown from horses dozens of times as a boy on ranches in Mexico. And the hill was covered with soft tufted grass that would make the landing not too painful.

No, I perceived, it wasn't all grass. A hundred feet ahead I could see a boulder about a foot high, perfectly round. Just as a boy on a bicycle says, "I mustn't hit that tree," and then hits it, I found myself thinking, "I mustn't hit that rock." At that moment the pinto stopped abruptly. I somersaulted through the air and fell on my back. On the rock.

I lay stunned. My breath had left me, and when I tried to rise I found my legs wouldn't move. I fell back, my eyes staring at the brilliant Colorado sky.

The pinto continued racing down the hill to join the other horses at the film location. The wranglers recognized that the runaway was my horse, and a search began. They found me lying helpless on the slope, still so winded that I couldn't talk. Nor could I move my legs.

A car took me to the hospital in Durango, and every bounce on the mountain road filled my body with exquisite pain.

X rays were taken, and no fractures of the bones could be seen. Nor did there appear to be any damage to the spine. Yet I still couldn't move my legs. "A muscle spasm," the doctor diagnosed. "As soon as the muscle relaxes, you'll be all right."

I remained in great pain the next day, but I felt movement returning to the right leg. It was numb, but I could move it. There was no feeling in the left leg, and it remained useless.

With each day the paralysis diminished in both legs, but the pain did not. By the fifth day my absence from the film company had become critical. Bill Wellman had shot all the scenes without me; unless I returned, the production would be forced to shut down. I returned. I was wound like an Egyptian mummy with adhesive tape, from my chest to my tailbone; I could be strapped only in areas covered by my skimpy Indian costume.

I felt secure in my white suit of armor, but when I took the first step, a spasm struck with excruciating pain and I fell to the hospital floor. The attendants lifted me back on the bed.

Another night of intense suffering. But in the morning I knew I had to go to work. Some of the tape that couldn't be hidden by the costume was removed. I was driven to the location, made up as an Indian brave, and placed before the camera. And despite the ice pick of pain that was driving into my backbone, I gave a performance.

Somehow I managed to get through the picture. Running was an impossibility, so my double performed the action scenes. But the climactic scene in *Across the Wide Missouri* could not be faked; that was the duel to the death between Gable and myself.

The script called for us to be stalking each other with muzzle-loading rifles. Gable realizes he must be able to refire swiftly, so he places the powder horn, the bullet, and the ramrod on the top of the log he is hiding behind. We both fire, and I realize that he must take the time to reload. So I throw away my rifle and charge at him with a knife. The suspense builds up as he furiously tries to reload his rifle before I can reach him. He can't finish in time, so he fires with the ramrod still in the barrel. The ramrod hits me as I almost reach him, and I fall dead.

"Okay, action!" Bill Wellman called, and I hurled myself toward Gable as the camera turned. When I fell to the ground, I felt as if I would never get up again.

The picture finished, and I returned to Los Angeles for more medical examinations. No damage could be found, yet the pain continued and my left leg remained difficult to move. I was advised to exercise, then the leg would return to normal and the pain would disappear.

It never has. I went to gyms and exercised with weights, and the leg never improved. And pain has been my constant companion since that clear Colorado day in 1950.

Pain is with me when I open my eyes in the morning. It accompanies me throughout the day and remains when I go to sleep at night. It is impossible to find a comfortable position in bed; I have even tried water beds, with no relief. The discomfort varies. Sometimes it almost disappears when I am playing tennis. But if my opponent hits a low ball to my forehand, I can return it only with the greatest pain. Sometimes I let the ball pass. Of course I could avoid such pain by not playing tennis. But I love the game and I will not let my own discomfort interfere with it. Nor with my work. Recently I appeared in a film, *The Mark of Zorro*, which required a lot of fencing. I did it myself.

Sometimes a script calls for action I simply cannot do. Like running up a flight of stairs, or vaulting over a wall. When such occasions arise, I confer with the director. "Could I take the first few steps and then cut to a double?" I suggest, or, "How about shooting from a different angle so we can suggest the action without doing it?" There is always a way to manage without sacrificing any of the script values.

My friends all know about my problem and they no longer

question it. But strangers are surprised to observe my persistent limp, and they ask, "What happened—did you hurt your foot?" I appreciate their concern, but it becomes tiring after being asked four or five times a day, every day of my life. "Oh, I twisted my foot playing tennis," I often reply. A quick answer, however inaccurate, seems more humane, both for the questioner and me, rather than repeating the whole story.

I seek no relief for the pain. A couple of cocktails can bring relief, but they also make my left leg more relaxed, less alert, less easy to move. So I don't seek help from alcohol. Or pills. I'm afraid of pills. Sure, I could find relief, but what would the pills lead to? No, thanks, I'd rather take the pain.

After Georgie and I had become friends with Georgia and Carroll Rosenbloom, he noticed my leg problem when we played tennis. He was familiar with such injuries, being owner of the Los Angeles Rams pro football team. Carroll urged me to consult Dr. Robert Kerlan, the Rams physician and an expert in athletic injuries. I underwent a thorough examination with sophisticated scanning devices that hadn't been developed when I was injured. Dr. Kerlan said that my problem was caused by a pinprick hemorrhage in the spine. If the hemorrhage had been any larger, I would have been paralyzed from the waist down.

So I am a lucky man. I consider myself so, despite my constant companion. That pain has been instrumental in my life. It has taught me something I could never learn before: to accept the inevitable. When there is hope for a cure to a physical condition or a human situation, you struggle. Actors especially live on hope—that the next role will turn their careers around, etc.—and they find their dreams trampled again and again. Only when you accept reality can you avoid the devastating series of disappointments. I have been told that surgery would be dangerous and would probably not improve my condition. I accept that, and I live with pain.

Sometimes it vanishes. There are times when I become so

immersed in another identity that I forget the pain at my back. Actors are fortunate that way. They have some magic words that are the best painkiller available. Those words are: "Curtain going up!" and "Camera! Action!"

Two years after the fall in *Across the Wide Missouri*, I was flying through the air forty feet from the ground. People watching were amazed that I could do it. So was I. Without thinking twice about it, I was sailing from one trapeze to another, with only a rope net between me and the cement floor of Stage 30.

The movie was *The Story of Three Loves*, and the producer, Sidney Franklin, said it would be a big break for my career at MGM. I believed him. Franklin was one of the studio's most prestigious producers, and the film was an ambitious undertaking, with a stellar cast in three interconnected love stories. One starred James Mason and Moira Shearer, another Leslie Caron and Farley Granger, the third Pier Angeli and myself. The directors were Vincente Minnelli and Gottfried Reinhardt, the supporting players included Ethel Barrymore, Agnes Moorehead, Ricky Nelson, and Zsa Zsa Gabor.

"You're going to play a trapeze artist, Ricardo," the producer told me. "I'd like to get as much reality as possible, so I want you to actually train on the trapeze. Do you think you can do that, Ricardo?"

"Absolutely, Mr. Franklin," I said, not mentioning my injury from *Across the Wide Missouri*.

My teacher was a trapeze artist named Harold Voise, a veteran of the circus. Every day I reported to him and spent long hours learning the tricks of the trade. I swung out from the platform, kicked my legs to increase height, did a scissor kick and turned around on the trapeze, kicked again to gain height, then landed back on the platform. I did it in reverse, and I hung from my knees on the platform and caught Harold's wife as she flew from another trapeze. I could climb to the platform in a sitting position, using only my hands on the rope. Harold also taught me to land in the net. The trick was to reach maximum height and come to a dead stop, drop straight down, and land on the back, head straight back. When the bounce came, you are supposed to bring your head forward to a perpendicular position.

On one fall I looked up too soon. The head acts as a rotor, propelling the body in its direction, and my knees buckled, striking my chin. My teeth clamped together, gouging two small pieces of my tongue. I was rushed to the hospital bleeding like a stuck pig, my left shoulder in great pain. The tongue healed, but to this day bursitis in my left shoulder provides memory of that fall.

I went right back to the trapeze, working as hard as ever. My hands were masses of blisters, but that didn't matter. It felt good to be preparing myself for a role which had not only daring action but a sensitive love story. At last I could show American audiences what I could do.

I had been working out on the trapeze for a month when I received a telephone call one evening. It was early, but I was already in bed to rest up for an early workout the next day.

"Hello, Ricardo, this is Kirk Douglas."

"Hello, Kirk." I was surprised, since I knew him only casually.

"How are you?"

"I'm all right, Kirk."

"Listen, Ricardo, do you have your heart set on doing *The Story of Three Loves?*"

I had a sinking feeling. "Why do you ask?"

"Because MGM is negotiating with me to do the circus role. I know you were cast for it, and I know you've been training on the trapeze. But I'll be frank with you; I want very much to do a circus picture. I always have. It's a good part, and they're willing to pay my price. But I won't accept if you really want to play the part."

I was deeply touched. What an unselfish thing for an actor to do!

"Sure, I want to do the picture, Kirk—but not if they don't want me. You go ahead. You'll be wonderful in the part. But, Kirk—"

"Yes?"

"Don't tell the studio that we talked. I want to see how they're going to handle the situation."

I reported for the trapeze training the next day. Again I flew through the air, but my heart wasn't in it. I continued the following day, and the next, my morale at ground zero. Finally on the fifth day I was summoned to the office of one of the top executives, Benny Thau. Also there was Sidney Franklin, the producer of *The Story of Three Loves*.

They hemmed and hawed and finally got to the point. "Ricardo, there's been a development," the producer said. "You know, *Three Loves* is going to be an expensive picture. Now I happen to think that you'd be wonderful in it, but I have the opportunity to cast a big box-office star. It's possible I can get Kirk Douglas. A name like his would be good for business."

"Mr. Franklin," I began, "not long ago a woman working at our house turned out to be the wrong person for the job. My wife, Georgiana, just didn't have the heart to fire her, so she asked me to do it. It was one of the most difficult things I've had to do in my life. I sympathize with you. If it's hard for me to fire a maid, then I can imagine how hard it must be for you to fire me. I wish you luck with the picture."

Franklin beamed his relief.

"Ricardo, that's a marvelous attitude," he remarked. "I want you to know that I still believe you're an extremely talented actor. I promise I'm going to look for a script that is worthy of your talent."

Of course I never heard from him again.

"I'm sorry, Ricardo, but we're going to end your contract."

The words from Dore Schary dropped like a bombshell, and I can't remember hearing much more that he said in his execu-

tive office that day in 1953. It was something about how bad
the movie business had been since the advent of television, how
MGM was being forced to cut back on all contracts as they ex-
pired. The rest was lost as I struggled to grasp the import of
Schary's announcement.

For eight years, MGM had been my home, my refuge, my
citadel. Although I was not pleased with the parts I had been
given, still I was proud to be a member of the MGM family.
The Leo the Lion trademark remained the hallmark of quality,
even though the films were not the high caliber of the 1930s.
Every department—sound, makeup, costume, photography, etc.
—was staffed by the best professionals in the industry.

I knew the end was coming. The contract player list dwin-
dled every month as options came due. I had been one of the
lucky ones; my original seven-year contract had been extended
an extra year. Now it was over, I learned from Dore Schary,
who would himself become a casualty before long.

As I got into my car, I still felt numb. The full force of the
news didn't hit me until I was driving along the boulevard on
my usual route from the studio to my home. Then I became so
emotional I had to pull over to the curb and turn off the
motor.

"Get a hold of yourself, Ricardo," I told myself, but the emotion remained. I had never felt so alone in my life.

Gone was the publicity department that could work its
magic to make you famous not only in the United States, but
all over the world. I could feel the results wherever I traveled.

Gone was the weekly paycheck that permitted me to support
my wife and children in comfortable style. We had enjoyed a
standard of living that allowed a few luxuries. Would that be
possible now?

Gone was the career planning, the assurance that I would appear in three pictures a year. I wasn't always pleased with the
roles, but I knew I would be working, since the studio was paying my salary. Now there would be no one looking for roles for
me.

Alone! I regained my equilibrium, but the depression remained. I drove home, and with a long face, I told Georgiana
the sorrowful news.

"We'll manage," she said cheerfully. "We'll do whatever has
to be done. We can sell the house and move to a smaller
house. I can manage the housework by myself. We can handle
it. No problem."

Georgiana is like that in a crisis; she responds calmly while
I'm inclined to become emotional. While I appreciated her attitude, I still felt depressed. So much so that I went to bed
early, wanting to lose my troubles in sleep.

Of course I lay awake. I couldn't overcome the awful feeling
of aloneness. About nine o'clock, the telephone rang.

"Ricardo, this is Tony Martin."

"Hi, Tony, how are you?"

"Fine, just fine. Say, Ricardo—"

"Yes?"

"I want you to relax and enjoy your freedom. It's happened
to me before, being dropped by a studio, and always something
better came up. Same thing will happen to you, I know it.
Yeah, I realize it's tough being let go after eight years. But
what the hell, you've got your independence now, and you can
call your own shots. I know you'll do okay. You've got talent
that MGM never tapped. So you get a good night's sleep and
rest up for the best years of your life. I'll be watching your career, amigo. Good night."

I was too astounded to say more than "Good night." I presumed that Tony had learned the news from his wife, Cyd
Charisse. But although I had worked several times with Cyd, I
had never known Tony very well. Yet he had the thought-
fulness to telephone me when he knew my spirit needed boost-
ing. It was a warm, lovely moment in my life.

Another telephone call.

"Ricardo, this is Aggie Moorehead. I know you've left
MGM, and I've got something you might be interested in. I'm

going to direct *Don Juan in Hell,* the Shaw play that I did a few years ago with Charles Boyer, Charles Laughton, and Cedric Hardwicke. The new production is going on the road, one-nighters all over the country. Hard work, but rewarding. I'd like you to play Don Juan."

I was overwhelmed. "But, Aggie, I haven't appeared in a play since I was a boy."

"That's all right. It'll come back to you—with a little help from yours truly."

"But Don Juan! I saw the play. It's a heavy part."

"You can do it, I know you can. I've watched your work at MGM. The pictures weren't much good, but you were."

Again, Agnes Moorehead had not been a close friend. But she became one because of our association with *Don Juan in Hell.* She had so much faith in me that I was determined not to fail her.

First of all, I had to learn a long and difficult part. Aggie staged *Don Juan* as Laughton had in the original company, with the actors in evening clothes, standing at lecterns. Kurt Kasznar, Mary Astor, Reginald Denny, and I, who were the new company, had the script on the lecterns before us. There was the temptation to use the script as a security blanket, refreshing the memory now and then. I determined not to do that. If I was going to face a live audience again, I knew I must have the courage to work without the script.

The most difficult part was the antithetical speech, a series of double adjectives that provide Don Juan's jaded view of pleasure seekers:

> They are not beautiful; they are only decorated. They are not clean; they are only shaved and starched. They are not dignified; they are only fashionably dressed. They are not educated; they are only college passmen. They are not religious; they are only pew-renters. They are not moral; they are only conventional. They are not virtuous; they are only cowardly. They are not even vicious; they are only "frail." They

are not artistic; they are only lascivious. They are not prosperous; they are only rich. They are not loyal, they are only servile; not dutiful, only sheepish; not public-spirited, only patriotic; not courageous, only quarrelsome; not determined, only obstinate; not masterful, only domineering; not self-controlled, only obtuse; not self-respecting, only vain; not kind, only sentimental; not social, only gregarious; not considerate, only polite; not intelligent, only opinionated; not progressive, only factious; not imaginative, only superstitious; not just, only vindictive; not generous, only propitiatory; not disciplined, only cowed; and not truthful at all: liars every one of them, to the very backbone of their souls.

Aggie showed me a trick on how to close the speech. As soon as I said, "To the very backbone of their souls," I deliberately turned the page of the script in a dramatic gesture. I never failed to get applause at the end of the speech.

Don Juan in Hell was a leap forward for my career, and it demonstrates how necessity can become your ally. Probably I would not have attempted the play if I had not been dropped by MGM. It seemed beyond my capacity, an exercise in mental acrobatics, a challenge to diction, to projection. It required a clarity of thought to sustain an extremely complex character for a couple of hours.

Because of my need to survive as an actor, I plunged into the assignment. I was aware of the danger with the critics. They would have their knives poised for this Hollywood actor who presumed to take on one of Shaw's most magnificent characters.

To my delight, the critics everywhere were not only kind, they were extremely complimentary. Perhaps the most satisfying comment came from John Simon, the New York critic who has been known to grind actors into hamburger. After admitting he had considered me "a second-rate actor in third-rate films," he went on to give me an accolade.

Something significant happened in a small town in Idaho.

We arrived by train late at night. There were no taxis at that hour, and the hotel was eight blocks away. I decided there was nothing to do but carry the bags myself.

By the time I arrived at the hotel, my shoulders were numb and my hands hurt from carrying the two suitcases. But somehow it was a pleasant hurt. There had been no limousine at the station, and there would be no flowers and fruit in a hotel suite. I no longer had the big-studio treatment. But I was earning my livelihood as an actor and doing something that was worthy and gratifying. At last I was self-sufficient.

Kyoto, Japan.

It was my first day of work in *Sayonara*, the James Michener story that Josh Logan was directing, with Marlon Brando as star. I was playing an actor of the Kabuki theater, and for weeks I had trained and rehearsed so I could duplicate the intricate movements of the Japanese actors. My first scene was to be in a theater, performing a traditional role in the guise of a woman. The audience was composed of Japanese extras, plus a few American actors, including Brando.

My makeup took hours to apply. The Japanese were meticulous in their techniques, using the fingernail to break the line of the painted eyebrow so it looks like hair. The wig was applied to my head, and I put on the heavy kimono. I looked in the mirror and wanted to cry. I was supposed to resemble a beautiful woman, but I thought I looked grotesque and ugly. I was certain the audience would start laughing the minute I stepped onto the stage.

The Japanese audience didn't laugh. The people merely sat motionless, their faces pleasant but inscrutable. My eyes darted from one to another, hoping for some sign of approval. Nothing.

Josh Logan put me through a rehearsal of a part of the dance, then called for a take. The cameras rolled, and I danced. "Cut," said Josh. "Now let's do the next part."

I studied the audience for a reaction. There was none. Had I failed? Were they too polite to laugh at me? I felt lonely in a strange land.

Marlon, who had been sitting in the audience with Patricia Owens, who played his sweetheart, left his seat and came onstage to talk to me.

"You, with all your Mexican machismo, I'll bet you feel ridiculous," he said.

"If you only knew, Marlon!" I sighed.

"I think I know," he replied. "Look, Ricardo, I've been watching you. You're doing a good job. The only way to do it is to go full-out. Don't be self-conscious. Go all the way, just as you've been doing. It's a good piece of work. Keep it up."

He returned to his seat, and I continued my performance with added confidence. The same audience returned the following day for the climax of the dance. I first portrayed a woman with a lion's mask, then the mask came to life and invaded the woman's body. She went offstage and returned as a lion. The last part was easier for me because of the strong movements, and I finished in a state of elation. The audience remained silent.

Finally Josh called for a long shot from the rear of the theater. I performed the dance once more, and Josh called "Cut!" Then he added, "It's all over, Ricardo. How does it feel to have done a good job?"

Before I could answer, all of the Japanese in the audience arose and gave me a cheering ovation. It was one of the great moments of my professional life.

Acting is the only profession that approaches being godlike, because it creates life. Of course the writer is the most important element in the dramatic process, being the initial force; for that reason I have always maintained the greatest respect for the author's lines. But then the actor, with the guidance of the director, must give the character the human qualities that will establish life.

Because of his unique position, the actor requires a special fortitude to withstand criticism. The critic tells the painter, "I didn't like your painting." Or the author, "I didn't like your book." But the critic tells the actor, "I didn't like *you*." It takes guts to place your persona on the line every time you step on a stage or before a camera.

I've had good help along the way. My first inspiration was Miss Araxi Jamgochian at Fairfax High School. She gave me the fundamentals—how to get on- and offstage, how to address the audience, etc.

Next came Tallulah Bankhead. Being as green as I could be, I was awed by watching such a total professional. Since I had a small part in her play, I had plenty of time to observe her from the wings. Whatever her offstage peccadilloes may have been, she treated the stage as a sacred temple.

"Remember this, young man," she told me, "professionalism must go hand in hand with acting. Otherwise it's all a sham."

Seki Sano gave form and substance to my instincts as an actor. When I did an improvisation in his class, he would stop me and say, "You are not giving us *the truth*. It is easy to overwhelm an audience with histrionics. But the essence of acting is truth, the simplicity of truth."

He had his students work in the accents and dialects of regions of Mexico, but even though they sounded strange, he insisted on clarity. "Think of the beauty, the sensuousness of the language," he insisted. "Words are the tools with which you express yourselves. Those tools are useless if the audience has to strain to hear what you say."

Years later when I was appearing in *Jamaica*, I was an observer for about three months at The Actors Studio in New York. I was impressed by the classes I saw, but I detected differences from the teachings of Seki Sano. Perhaps I was wrong, but it seemed to me that the New York actor was *using* his fellow actor. Seki Sano insisted that we *give* to the other actor, not use him. In giving we would receive.

Jamaica was directed by Bobby Lewis, later a teacher at Yale University. He provided an acronym of essentials for actors that I have found useful: THEC. The initials stand for Truth, Humor, Energy, and Clarity. It is an oversimplification, but a helpful reminder. Kurt Kasznar, with whom I toured in *Don Juan in Hell,* made an addition: THECL. The *L* standing for Love.

Learning movie technique was not terribly difficult. The stage is a long shot; you must project to reach your audience. A movie close-up is like being under a microscope. You think loudly, but you show little action. Too much would make you seem grotesque.

MGM was the ideal training ground for a film actor. Everything at the studio was done with a high degree of professionalism, and the same was expected of actors. So we learn the nuances of lighting, how to hit our marks smoothly, how to perform intricate movements and remain within camera range. Often today when I complete a complicated scene without mishap, a fellow alumnus of the studio will comment, "That's the MGM training."

MGM provided training of all kinds for actors. There were singing and dancing lessons, and dramatic coaching by Lillian Burns. I also had sessions with Gertrude Fogler, a voice coach who was an expert on accents. She aimed not to eradicate my accent entirely, but to make sure that my speech was understood by American audiences. She told me not to speak Spanish at all, and I followed her instructions. That may have helped my English, but I regretted it later, because I didn't raise my children bilingually.

Looking at my film career, I'm afraid that I haven't accomplished much. Part of that was because I simply wasn't cast for the starring roles that the American actors got. Partly it was a lack of direction. As I study some of the films on the late, late show, I wish that I had received more help from directors.

I've known a few who have been helpful—John Sturges, Sidney Lumet, Martin Ritt. Martie directed *Adventures of a Young Man*, which was based on Ernest Hemingway's early life. I was cast as a World War I Italian major, counterpart to the role that Vittorio de Sica played in *A Farewell to Arms*.

We were filming in Verona, and Martie called a rehearsal in the picturesque hotel where we were staying. Richard Beymer, Susan Strasberg, Eli Wallach, and I were there. I started reading my part, and Martie interrupted me.

"Ricardo," he said, "if I had wanted Vittorio de Sica, I would have gotten Vittorio de Sica."

Martie was right. I had seen De Sica in the other role, and I was trying to give the same intensity. That is my failing. I am demonstrative in nature, as you will learn from friends who accompany me to football games and prizefights. I'm inclined to approach roles a bit too flamboyantly, and that's why I need a director who will help me to simplify, simplify, simplify.

I know there are some actors who resent direction, believing it to be a criticism of their work. They are guarded and insecure. I don't say I'm secure, but I know that once a performance is on film, nothing can change it. So I welcome all the direction I can get.

Returning to the stage after a dozen years in the studios of Mexico and MGM was no great problem for me. I liken it to playing tennis, a game I much enjoy. When you are trying to develop a stroke, you often go from bad to worse until finally you reach a point when the stroke begins to come more easily. Then you go on a trip and return to tennis after a few weeks. Suddenly the stroke seems to work perfectly. But after a set or two, you become self-conscious of the stroke and it turns bad again.

My first Broadway show after leaving MGM was *Seventh Heaven*, in 1955. It was a lovely play, with a beautiful score by

Victor Young and a talented cast including Gloria DeHaven, Robert Clary, Kurt Kasznar, and Bea Arthur. But unfortunately the show failed to please the New York critics. I worked hard during the five weeks of rehearsals, but it was rough going. By the time we opened in New Haven, I had the part pretty well under control. But then I started analyzing things and asking myself, "What would Seki Sano say?" I became aware of my stroke, and the New York opening was nerve-wracking. I had to learn once more to forget technique and let the performance flow.

In 1963 I was appearing in *Cheyenne Autumn*, directed by John Ford. It was my first and only picture with the great director, and I approached it with great anticipation, and some trepidation. Other actors had told me about Ford's tendency to pick someone in the company as a kind of patsy and kid him unmercifully throughout the shooting. So I was wary.

During the early days on location in the Rockies, I believed that my fears were groundless. I felt nothing but radiations of affection from Ford. Then one day I was doing a prairie scene for which he gave directions in an offhanded manner:

"Now I wantcha to face the camera and look at something over there, see? Then ya turn back and give the order, whatever the hell it is, turn back and walk out of camera left. Let's shoot it."

The camera rolled and I looked in the direction he indicated, turned and delivered the line, then faced the camera and started to move out of the scene.

"CUT!" Ford bawled. "For crissake, when you turn, turn away from the camera! Away from the camera! Do you think we want to see your face all the time? The trouble with you is you're doing too much television."

It seemed to me the offense didn't rate the bawling out, and so I replied, "Mr. Ford, if you would give me more jobs in your

pictures, I wouldn't have to do television." He never kidded me
again.

A working actor must work, and so I and most of my col-
leagues have had jobs we would like to forget. My first picture
after I left MGM was something terrible I made in Italy with
Rhonda Fleming, *The Courtesan of Babylon.* I knew it was
going to be a stinker, but what could I do? The producers
agreed to pay my regular price, and I had a wife and four children to support. If I had been a single man, I could have sold
my house, moved into an apartment, and tightened my belt
until a good role came along.

I've had dry periods of six or seven months when I could find
absolutely nothing. Twice I had to take second mortgages on
my home, which I hated to do because I don't like to be a bor-
rower. At such times I didn't panic. I had an understanding
wife and helpful friends, and I simply waited until a job came
along. I was one of the lucky ones: I survived. A great many actors—and some excellent ones—simply disappeared from the
scene in those lean years after the movie studios went bust and
before television picked up the slack.

I've done some rotten roles. A few I will turn down—if the
subject matter is degrading, if the material is demeaning to
Mexico. I have no qualms about playing a murderer, an adulterer, a dope pusher—as long as the script doesn't say that it is
good to be a murderer, adulterer, dope pusher. I'll play anything, unless the intent of the role goes against my moral judg-
ment.

No experience is wasted. The main thing is to *act.* Even if
you realize you can do little with the character. Even if you
know the critics are going to spit on the production. I don't
mean you should "take the money and run." I hate that expression. What I mean is that out of the worst movie, stage play,
or television show might come a positive experience that will
contribute to the totality of your development.

I don't consider any work I have done to be wasted. Even

The Courtesan of Babylon. Every experience contributes new data to the computer mind.

And so I prepare for each new role as if it were the most important of my career. That's not always easy in television, which lacks the luxury of rehearsal and preparation that theater and feature films provide. Often I receive a script the day before the start of production.

"Go to Western Costume this afternoon and pick out your wardrobe," I am told. "The call tomorrow is 6:30 A.M. You'll be doing scenes 128, 193, 194, 195, 2A, 2B, and 7."

I have already read the script through once at normal speed, without pausing over my own lines. That would be a mistake because I don't know the character yet. I want to know and understand him and study his relationship to the other characters and the action. The first impression of a character in a script, just as in real life, is not always correct.

After the first reading, I concentrate on the totality of the situation, then I start to zero in on my character. Was my first impression of him correct? I read the script again, and now I start to notice more things about him. His faults, and his virtues, too. Even a villain must have virtues, otherwise he is a caricature. Likewise a character can be so benign as to be unbelievable.

If I have enough time, I read the script six times. By then I am familiar enough with the character that it doesn't matter if we shoot out of sequence. I could perform the last scene first and still retain a firm grasp on the action. After six readings, my part is pretty well memorized, and I begin to work on specifics. Even if the company shoots entirely different scenes tomorrow, I will be prepared.

The role may take three days or three weeks, then I move to another one. And if one doesn't come along, I'll go out on the road with a play. Fortunately, I'm at the point where my age and experience fill a need. I'm prepared to do anything— movies, television, stage, commercials, records, whatever. I've heard of a top executive who was asked the secret of his success. Without blinking an eye he replied, "The fact that I have not only accepted but welcomed responsibility." I feel the same way in my profession. I not only accept but welcome challenge.

SUNDAY

Another refreshing night's sleep. I awoke to the sound I have heard all weekend: the chugga-chugga-chugga of the Rainbird sprinklers as they swept over the endless rows of potted plants at the nursery that surrounds Manresa.

I began to feel like a longtime resident. The pressures of an acting career, of deadlines and last-minute script changes, of crowded freeways and business appointments were far away. I was absorbed in the quietude of that blessed place. I also felt like a longtime companion, even a friend, to my fellow retreatants, though we have not spoken to each other. In silence it is easier to read the attitudes, the actions of other people.

Little courtesies seem larger when words do not intrude. I noticed that when the servings were small, one of the men put a small portion on his plate; he wanted to make sure that the others at the table would have enough to eat.

The attitudes in chapel are revealing. One boy fidgeted through the talks and the services; you got the impression that he would have preferred to spend his weekend on a surfboard at the Pacific. Another boy about the same age listened intently to everything that was said; he reminded me of my own seriousness in church at his age.

The approaches to prayer provided a revealing study. The retreat captain—the man who organized the weekend, arranged transportation, etc.—was very businesslike. He was the first to kneel, and he led the liturgy in a firm, clear voice. A take-charge guy. Another man knelt slowly, thoughtfully, and he read the replies in the prayer book as though he were discovering them for the first time.

David, my young tablemate, continued to be the last to arrive at chapel. He hobbled through the door, with an apologetic look on his face, then knelt slowly, painfully, and became totally immersed in prayer.

The retreatants faced a full schedule for the last day:

7:00 Rise

7:30 Morning Prayers

7:45 Breakfast

9:00 Conference in Chapel

10:30 Rosary

11:00 Conference in Chapel

12:00 Examination of Conscience in Chapel

12:15 Lunch

1:30 Conference in Chapel

2:00 Celebration of the Eucharist—Renewal of Baptismal Vows—Papal Blessing, etc.

2:45 Coffee and Farewell in Dining Room

I tried to immerse myself in the devotions, and most of the time I succeeded. Not always. It was inevitable that the actor in me would emerge from time to time.

The Rosary was a touching part of the Sunday events. Father Brannon led us through the garden, using a small portable microphone so the words could be heard by all of the retreatants. As we walked along, he handed the mike to each of us in turn and we recited the Rosary.

When the mike was placed in my hand, I suddenly reverted. Perhaps I was influenced by what we had heard at Saturday dinner: a recording of Laurence Olivier reading the parables in highly dramatic style.

"Hail Mary, full of grace," I began, as though I were acting a scene in a movie, "the Lord is with Thee; blessed art Thou amongst women and blessed is the fruit of thy womb, Jesus."

The next man in line took the mike with a hand that was calloused from a lifetime of work. "Hail Mary, full of grace . . ." he began, and I was immediately struck by the simple earnestness of his entreaty. He made my own prayer seem shallow and superficial.

Finally Father Brannon gave the microphone to David. All of us listened with apprehension as he stammered through the prayer: "Hail Mary . . . full of grace . . . the Lord is with Thee . . . blessed are Thou among women. . . ."

It seemed like minutes before he finished. Listening to him had been a painful yet uplifting experience. Surely his was the prayer dearest to Mary.

My thoughts on the retreat weekend quite naturally flowed to my own children.

They had arrived in a fairly regular pattern: Laura, Mark, and Anita at two-year intervals, followed by Victor, three years later. Laura had been a difficult delivery for Georgiana, because her doctor at that time didn't believe in medication during childbirth. Mark had been easier, and the last two were simple. But we faced a potential danger with Anita and Victor because of blood type. Doctors discovered that Georgiana was RH negative and I was weak positive. The hospital took no chances with Anita; she was put in an incubator immediately, with a total transfusion ready if needed. I went to see her right afterward. I had never seen a newborn baby that had not been cleaned, and I gazed down at what looked to me like a piece of liver. I fell to my knees and almost fainted. Fortunately, the nurse helped me to my feet and administered a medicinal shot of brandy.

I found fatherhood to be an uplifting experience. Of necessity you become less self-centered, less selfish. You must think about the mother and the child and what you can do for them as a husband and father. You make all kinds of resolves, some of which you keep.

My only regret is that we started our family so early. Georgiana and I scarcely had a chance to become acquainted before we were plunged into parenthood. We were too young. We made mistakes. I'm certain we could have done a better job as parents if we had been more mature. But we weren't, and so we had to function out of instinct—and on the basis of our own upbringings.

To the end of my life I will never forget the day I brought Laura and Georgiana home from the hospital. I was quite young, and the sight of the little creature cradled in my wife's arms gave me chills. Partly that was due to pride, I suppose, the feeling that every parent gets with a newborn child. Perhaps it is a sense of continuation of self, a natural human instinct.

I was also scared. That tiny creature who was my daughter seemed so fragile. I was almost afraid to pick her up, for fear that I might bruise her. Soon I learned that baby was a lot tougher than she looked. And Georgiana and I had the services of a trained nurse to help us break in as parents.

As the baby grew, so did my love for her. I realized that I would make any sacrifice for her. But I also realized that I had certain responsibilities, and I needed to learn about them. So, like every other parent in America, I read Dr. Spock. He didn't turn me on. I respect his knowledge and achievements, and I'm sure his teachings have been helpful for many, many parents. But not for me.

I was a father to my daughter, I reasoned, not a friend. She would have many friends in her life, but only one father and only one mother. I realized that my function was totally different from that of a friend. I was to be a teacher—mainly through example. I was to be the protector—I was willing to give my life for her.

Painful though it was to us, Georgiana and I began very early to discipline the child. If we had visitors and Laura entered the room and demanded our attention, we said, "No, you must not interrupt." She had to learn respect for others. In time she knew that she should enter the room and wait until one of us said, "Yes, dear, what is it?"

Does that sound severe? I believe that our children seemed more secure and happier. At bedtime they would come into the living room in their pajamas and robes, looking like little dolls. When we said it was time to go to bed, they would kiss us good night and go up the stairs singing. We felt so proud of them, and I believe they felt that pride and love.

That contrasted with the homes of other couples we visited. Often the mother said, "Come on, dear, it's time to go to bed." The child answered, "I don't wanna go to bed," and launched into a fit of screaming and kicking the floor. Finally the mother had to carry the child up the stairs.

It seemed to me that the other kind of discipline made the child freer and happier. And so we continued the road—discipline, good manners, clean habits, neat dress. This was not always easy for my children to accept, especially as they developed friends with a different kind of upbringing.

"But Barbara's father lets her stay out until two o'clock," my daughter might say. "Why can't I?"

"Because I am not Barbara's father," I would reply. "I am Ricardo Montalban. We have our own standards here, Barbara's family has theirs. I'm not saying they're wrong. I have my own belief of what is right for us."

"Why do I have to cut my hair?" my son would ask. "Everybody's wearing it long these days."

"But you're not everybody," would be my reply. "As long as you live in this house, you follow the rules. When you have your own house, then you can make your own rules. In this house we do not have a democracy. Forget it. You did not vote for me. I didn't campaign to be your father. We are father and son by the grace of God, and therefore I accept that great privilege and awesome responsibility. In accepting it I am *going* to perform the role as father. Not as a friend or pal. Our ages are too different; I can't play with you as a pal. We can share many things eventually, but we are not friends. I am much more than a friend—twenty times, a hundred times what a friend is. I'm your father, which includes being a friend, but on a level that is entirely different. Therefore, we will do in this house as I say. If you know that my intent is dictated by love—and that you cannot question because I do love you more than my own life—then my decisions will be not easy to take, but easier. So know that I love you, and know that my intent is unquestionable. The application of that intent might be erroneous because of what I'm lacking in intelligence."

I think—or I like to think—that the message was loud and clear and they understood it. Both Georgiana and I are affectionate by nature, I believe, and so they should have felt very much loved, if very much disciplined.

This kind of attitude had to be established from the cradle. The authority had to be complete and consistent, but overlying it was the feeling of love. This I was not acting; it came from the gut. And since that love was instinctive and pervading, the child could sense it without being told, "Daddy loves you."

Rebellion? Of course there were signs of it. That is only natural, not just among human beings but in the animal kingdom. I like to go to the zoo and observe how the animals behave. Especially the lion cubs. At first they're just like kittens. As they start to grow, they are filled with energy and vitality, and they roll around with each other. The older lions sit blinking in the sun, ignoring the playful cubs.

As the cubs grow older, one of them starts taunting the old lion. He bites the lion's tail, swats him on the back, growing more and more daring. The cub is testing, testing, seeing how far he can go. Finally he faces up to the lion and swats him on the face. The old lion lets out a roar and whacks the cub with a paw, sending him head over heels.

That, I believe, is part of the design for the continuation of the species. The young lion continues testing and taunting the old one until finally he takes over the pride. That's the way nature goes.

The same with human beings. Children start to question their father, they want to do things better than their father, they compete with their father. I don't resent their questioning me, I'm not insulted by their rebellious attitudes. I think that's only normal. But it's also normal for me to want to maintain discipline and control until such time as children become responsible adults and can take over.

To maintain control, it is essential that husband and wife work in concert. Fortunately, Georgiana and I had the same attitude on how children should be brought up. So there was no chance for a child to ask one parent a favor that had been denied by the other.

One day I was visiting a friend when his daughter came screaming into the living room. "What's the matter, darling?" said the father, sweeping the girl into his arms.

"Mommy spanked me!" said the child.

"Bad Mommy," said the father. "Mommy's mean to my little darling."

I realized immediately that child was in for trouble. Perhaps the marriage, too. With two parents pulling in opposite directions, that girl had to grow up confused. If her parents were united on her discipline, she might resent being punished, but she would not be torn apart by the divided loyalty.

I hope I haven't created the impression that Georgiana and I were model parents. We weren't. As I've mentioned, we started our family when we were very young, and we had our share of sorrows as well as joys. I'm sure it wasn't easy for our children to grow up in a time when most of their friends and classmates were being reared in an entirely different way. This was especially noticeable in neighborhoods where people enjoyed considerable means.

My children, thank God, have never known want. But, although I have earned a comfortable living during most of my Hollywood years, Georgiana and I did not lavish material things on our children, the way many of our neighbors did. For them it was a never-ending spiral from fancy bicycles to motor scooters to small cars to ever bigger and more expensive cars.

From a very early age, my children had to earn their allowances by performing certain duties. The job might have been simple, like sweeping the front steps. We could afford help, so they really didn't have to assist in the housekeeping. But I felt they had to earn certain things in life, otherwise what was given to them would have no value. The boys also delivered on paper routes and worked at the local market to earn extra money.

Laura, Mark, Anita, and Victor faced a hazard that most other children did not have. Their father was not a stockbroker or an accountant or a truck driver. He was a well-known actor —and from Mexico. I don't believe children are basically cruel, but they do make quick, harsh judgments about anyone who seems different. And so I know that my sons and daughters endured taunts like, "So you think you're a big shot because your old man is a movie star!" And the name—Montalban. So different and foreign-sounding to American kids. They made fun of it in unkind and thoughtless ways.

I'm sure that some of my children's friends made fun of my accent, which was much more pronounced in the years when my children were growing up. I learned that a student in their school was the butt of jokes because of an accent.

"I know that television comedians make fun of accents," I told my children, "and there is humor in it—if it is done with love. But if it is done merely to put down the person with an accent, then it is wrong. After all, why does he have an accent? Because he is speaking a language he is not familiar with. He can speak *two* languages, and that's something not many people can do. So, unless you can speak both his languages better than he does, you shouldn't criticize him."

My children no doubt were stigmatized by some unthinking playmates because their father was a Mexican, as if that were something to be ashamed of. They never complained to me about this, or any of the other taunts by other children. I'm sure they didn't want to hurt me, and I take that as an expression of love and respect. I heard about such things from their teachers and other parents.

I tried to prepare my children by telling them, "You know, individuality is a wonderful thing, a great gift. How terrible it would be if we all had the same fingerprints, the same faces, the same voices. It would be the dullest, most boring kind of world imaginable. Personal identity should be one of your most prized possessions. Cherish it in yourself, and in others, too."

Happily, all four of our children did develop their own individualities. Even though they stemmed from the same parents and grew up in the same environment, their personalities and temperaments differ in fascinating ways. They are independent-minded, but they were able to escape the conformism of many others in a generation that was supposedly nonconformist.

I once had an encounter with what was known as the Love Generation. That was a few years ago when the hippies invaded the Sunset Strip in blue jeans and bare feet. I had finished a morning rehearsal, and having had no breakfast, I stopped at the original Hamburger Hamlet for an early lunch.

Being in a hurry, I sat down at the counter and ordered a hamburger. Sitting next to me was a young man, shoeless, and so untrimmed and unshaved that everything he ate seemed to turn into hair. He stared at me for a while and then he said, "Hey, man, aren't you what's-his-name?"

"That's right," I replied. "I *am* what's-his-name."

"Crazy, man. Hey, I see you, and you know where it's at, you know? You're not menopause."

"Thank you," I said dubiously, returning to my hamburger.

Another young man came in and sat down on the stool on my other side. He was an exact replica of the other one—same hair, same beard, same bare feet. It turned out they knew each other, and the first one said, "Say, man, look who's here. You know—what's-his-name."

No. 2 glanced at me and said, "Yeah! Groovy! Man, you're okay."

I listened to them expound on peace, brotherhood, and love as I finished my hamburger, then I asked the waitress for the check and started to leave.

"Peace," said No. 1, lifting his two fingers.

"Love," said No. 2, giving the same sign.

I probably should have paid the bill and left, but I couldn't resist making a comment.

"What is it you mean by love?" I asked. "I wonder if it doesn't mean that you love yourself. Let me tell you something. I am eating a hamburger that has onions, ketchup, mayonnaise, meat, and bread. The reason that I am chewing with my mouth closed is not because it is immoral or illegal to chew with my mouth open. I keep my mouth closed out of love for you, because it is not a very pleasant sight to watch the food being mixed with saliva. All good manners are motivated by love for your neighbor. Look at you, slobbering all over your beard; it is not a pleasant sight. So you don't love me, because you're really taking my appetite away.

"Now out of the love for you, I was eating my hamburger with my elbows very close to my sides as I brought the hamburger up to my mouth. Don't move—look where you are. See —you are sprawled all over and intruding on my little area where I have a right to be free. So again, I love you, you don't love me.

"Also this morning, out of the love for you, I took a shower so I could smell clean. But you two do not smell clean. In fact, you have a very pungent odor that really interfered with my enjoyment of the hamburger. So again, let's set this straight: I love you, you don't love me."

They looked stunned for a moment, and then they smiled. At least I think they were smiling behind all that hair.

"Hey, cool, man!" said No. 1.

"Groovy, ya know?" said No. 2.

They took it so well that as I left the restaurant I regretted having made the outburst.

I don't know whether I was a good father. I don't know whether I'm a good actor, although I try. I'm sure that in some instances I made terrible mistakes with my children. But they were honest mistakes.

"You should certainly judge my faults," I told my sons and daughters. "You should certainly question my logic. You may even question my decisions or my intelligence. But what you cannot really question is my intent. My intent is to guide you, to the best of my ability, in directions that will ultimately culminate in your happiness. It's as simple as that."

Looking back now, I have one regret. Well, perhaps it's not a regret, but something I question. That was my decision to try to steer my children away from show business.

My feeling was based on the harsh reality about the chance of success in the entertainment business. Over and over again I stressed the precarious nature of acting careers, and perhaps that deterred them from entering related fields, such as music. I think Victor might have had the talent, the temperament, and maybe the inclination to be an actor. Anita might have done well in music. But none of the children has entered show business. Perhaps I was wrong in being so negative, but my intent was to avoid having them hurt.

You can't live your life over again. So you figure you did it to the best of your ability. I don't say that I raised my children well, but I did as well as I was able. Whether it was a good or bad job, only God can tell me someday.

"What do you think about the women's rights movement, Ricardo?"

I was asked that question on a television talk show. Here is what I replied:

"Nothing in the world is constant, everything is in a state of flux. New thoughts appear, out of a natural evolution. Women's lib is a consequence of that evolution.

"What does women's lib mean? I don't have the expertise or the intelligence to understand it thoroughly. But if it means that woman is a creature under God, on equal terms with man, of course. Certainly. That's self-evident. If it means she has equal rights, of course. If it means 'equal pay for an equal job,' of course. It means all those things in areas where woman deserves equality with man. If the movement exists because there hasn't been that parity, because it has been an unjust situation, then I am totally for it.

"However, there is use and abuse, and I believe that some movements can become abusive and they can become ridiculous at times. If women's lib means that a woman is going to lose her femininity, as opposed to masculinity, then I am against it. Man and woman should compensate in their union, their lacks and their needs. Marriage between them should be a relationship of cooperation rather than competition. When couples compete, they destroy the very essence of masculinity and femininity.

"It is very sad for me to see that in their competition with men, women have given up their seat on the bus. Now the men remain seated and the women stand up. If women are competing with men, that extends to the seat on the bus.

"Many words have a tendency to disappear as we achieve so-called progress. Among them are chivalry . . . femininity . . . purity . . . innocence . . . morality . . . modesty. To me they are very beautiful words. I have the feeling that today they are considered old-fashioned; there is no longer a need for them. That saddens me.

"Male and female are two very important words to me. Unisex is not to me an attractive concept. Woman has been called 'the weaker sex,' but I think that is ludicrous. I believe woman is the stronger sex, because that's where life begins. Therefore that instrument is much healthier, stronger than the male. I have heard that in great disasters like the plague, the mortality between male and female babies is three to one. The female can withstand that kind of a test more readily, therefore that makes her stronger.

"The only area where man is stronger is in his muscle. In primitive society, that was useful to protect the family. But I think the woman has the mental and mercurial quality that can enwrap a man without his even knowing it. That is a quality that I believe is endowed by nature, just as the physical aspect is endowed by nature.

"In cave days, man could assert himself forcefully, drag his mate by the hair into the cave when she talked too much or whatever irritated him. Today I think there is a great frustration in man. I don't believe he can compete in an argument or a discussion with a woman. Women can be very persuasive; at times they seem illogical, but they are also clever and intuitive. In the vast number of cases, man doesn't have a chance in an argument.

"Since he can no longer use his muscle and often loses in argument, modern man has developed an uncertainty and bewilderment in how to cope with woman. I may be wrong, but this is what I have observed. Right or wrong, those are my thoughts.

"I believe that man and woman, endowed by nature with definite male and female traits, should be compatible and complementary to each other. Not *ever* in competition. That is the only fault I find in the women's movement."

Fortunately in our marriage, Georgiana and I have never considered ourselves to be in competition. We both have our realms: she is the homemaker, I am the home provider. We respect each other's preeminence in our particular realm. We don't compete, yet each of us contributes.

We started together with the same religion, and that was a help. It was one barrier we did not have to face. We also took our vows seriously: "for better for worse, for richer for poorer, in sickness and in health . . . forsaking all others, till death do us part." Sharing the same belief, we had the same moral concept of what marriage is. We believed you shouldn't make a mockery of your vows. Otherwise you should just shack up together, as is the custom today. The attitude is: "Well, honey, we'll see if it works. If it doesn't, see ya later."

Georgiana and I made a commitment. We *committed* ourselves to follow a certain course. And I must say that commitment has paid wonderful dividends.

Of course a marriage can face what seems to be an insurmountable problem. You feel like giving up. But—if you find an eventual solution through a common goal, a common dedication, then you can experience insurmountable joy. There is a compensation for everything you do in life.

I really don't like to be a quitter, and neither does Georgiana. That attitude has helped us resolve our differences. After all, we have different temperaments, and not just male and female. We sprang from different cultures. Our original languages were different. Our computer brains were fed very different information about social aspects. Such things can become a formidable barrier to climb.

Also consider the fact that we were very young and scarcely knew each other when we became husband and wife. I realize that might seem old-fashioned today. The attitude is: "Why not live together and see if it works out?" I respect that view, as I respect all sincere opinions. But I hope that my opinion isn't laughed at, either.

I like to have things develop naturally in life—spontaneously, without premeditation. When I felt such an attraction for Georgiana after knowing her only two weeks—not only a physical attraction but because of her character as well—I made the decision to marry her. I think it's very exciting and adventurous to go with that wonderful urge. The relationship never becomes stale because it's a constant challenge.

When we had been married three years, among our best friends were two couples who were constantly amazed by the fights that Georgiana and I had. One of the wives once asked me, "Do you mean to tell me that you and Georgiana have big arguments?"

"Ever since we got married," I replied. "We have our spats all the time."

"Isn't that strange?" she said. "We've been married four years now, and we have never, never had a harsh word between us."

The other husband and wife said the same thing. Both couples are divorced now.

Their kind of marriage made no sense to me. It's like a man who retires; very often he goes to seed. He lacks the challenge, the stimulation of his daily work. I think marriage is a daily challenge. It's that mountain that has to be climbed.

Georgiana and I still have our spats, but they are farther apart now and more short-lived. We are quicker to see how ridiculous our arguments are. Georgiana especially has a well-developed sense of humor. Very often a smile can wipe out all contention.

The outsider might consider that our marriage has been a difficult one because of my many absences. An actor must go where the work is. After we had been married twenty years, Georgiana and I totaled the time I had been away from home because of movie locations and stage tours. It came to seven years!

That sounds terrible, and yet those separations were very good for us. They were not separations out of choice; I had to work, and Georgiana had to stay home with the children. We accepted that. The coming home was a great joy. Somehow in absence you recall more virtues in your partner, become less aware of the daily irritations. It's trite but true: absence makes the heart grow fonder.

During our early squabbles, there was never any thought of separation. Neither of us packed our bags and left in a huff. That doesn't mean that one of us didn't seek fresh air to cool off. Sometimes I would get in the car and take a drive to conquer my anger. And Georgiana would run complaining to her mother, Gladys Belzer.

My mother-in-law is one of the most brilliant women I have ever met. She was a forerunner of women's lib, freethinking, creative, intelligent.

"Ricardo is impossible," Georgiana complained to her mother. "He wants to be the boss. He thinks we should have a patriarchal society because the Bible says a woman should cling to her husband. I don't think that's right. Is he the boss, Mama?"

"Of course he is, dear," Mrs. Belzer replied, pausing before she added, "*when* he is right."

Children are a great responsibility, and after we had had four, Georgiana and I decided we should stop for a while. How to stop? If you are a Catholic, you use the rhythm system, which consists of abstaining from intercourse during the forty-eight-hour period of the wife's ovulation. That is the amount of time when the woman can be impregnated.

In some cases, as with Georgiana, there can be an irregularity of menstrual periods. So for four months she had to take her temperature every morning before she got out of bed. Then she took the charts to the doctor, and he compiled the information to calculate her earliest and latest time of ovulation. Just to be certain, he suggested that we should refrain from sex one day before and one day after.

That meant abstaining twelve days out of every month. What happened to us after four children and eight years of marriage was interesting. Perhaps it's because if you can have something any time you want it, your appetite is lessened. I found that by abstaining for those twelve days, it was like a renewal of the honeymoon every month. The interruption added something to the physical relationship that was not there before. There was a renewal of excitement and anticipation.

We continued using the rhythm system for a number of years, and then we decided we might like to have one more child. For some reason we never did.

I personally am glad that we abided by the rhythm system. It added a certain romanticism to our marriage. And we were following the Catholic teaching, which is that you should not interfere with the natural function of planting the seed in the woman. Once the seed is planted, it should follow its natural course. When you abstain, you are not really frustrating the natural function. That, in a very simplistic way, is what it's all about.

Abstinence is a way of renovating many feelings that cease to have the same importance or excitement when they become customary.

Now we are alone.
To a couple with only one child, I'm sure it can be a very

traumatic experience when the child leaves home. Since we had four children, we were weaned from parenthood. They left one at a time. When one left, we had three remaining as shock absorbers. By the time the last one moved out, we had already had three lessons on the departure of children. The last one was easier to bear.

In the beginning it was lonely. You miss them a great deal. Not only the love, which comes from the gut. Also the little sounds, the laughter, the music.

But with the passing of time, I have discovered for the first time a new aspect in my relationship with Georgiana. That is: *privacy.*

I do believe Georgiana and I are getting to know each other better. We are sharing something wonderful and new. Instead of moping about the children who are gone, we find life exciting.

The freedom is delightful. Supposing we're visiting friends' house and they say, "Why don't you stay the night?" We can say, "Sure—why not?" We could never have done that before. Now we have total freedom in discussing things. Even the freedom to caress each other intimately and fully without being on the lookout for the children.

This new life of ours reinforces my theory about accepting each moment as it comes. If you don't live in the past and don't look for the future, life can be an ever-changing, multifaceted, and rewarding experience. I've never been bored with life. Maybe that's because I've never been bored with Georgiana.

Of course we miss the children. Fortunately, three of them live in the Los Angeles area, so we can see them; our firstborn, Laura, lives in New York, and we miss her terribly. We have seen them all grow. They are adults; they have their own lives. In many areas my children are more educated, more knowledgeable than I am, more aware of the times. But I have traveled farther, and I know where the dangerous turns in the road are. I can still provide guidance.

Let me tell you about seeing our first grandchild.

Georgiana and I went to New York with our daughter Anita. They came from Los Angeles, I arrived from a film location. My plane got to New York first, and I went to the Hotel Lombardy, a short distance from Laura's apartment. I didn't call her or go there, because I didn't want to deny Georgiana or myself the pleasure of seeing our grandchild together for the first time. The baby was named Georgiana in her grandmother's honor.

Georgiana and Anita arrived about two hours after I did, and neither stopped to unpack. "Let's go!" Georgiana insisted.

As we walked along the Manhattan street, I pondered in my mind what the scene would be like in motion picture terms. All I could see was diffusion around the edges, soft colors, the angelic little child dressed in fluffy pink. I could see myself taking little Georgie into my arms with angels singing and the sky filled with a beautiful rainbow.

"Mom! Dad! Anita!" Laura greeted us all with hugs and kisses.

"Where's the baby?" I asked.

"Right this way."

We went to the nursery and saw the little four-month-old doll. Georgiana took her up and placed a cheek against hers and started to cry. I didn't cry. I completely broke down, making deep sobbing noises like an idiot. What a greeting for my poor frightened granddaughter.

I started smoking when I was nineteen, to my parents' dismay. My mother didn't smoke at all, my father only a Sunday cigar. They realized that tobacco wasn't good for me, and they hoped I would at least wait until I was twenty-one before I started. But I got involved in the theater, and it was the big thing for actors to smoke. You bought yourself a fancy lighter, whipped it out, and lighted a cigarette in the suave manner of William Powell. A wonderful prop.

Smoking seemed to help consume my excess of nervous energy, and by the time I was appearing in *Jamaica*, I was a two-pack-a-day man. I had to have one while I was making up, before I went onstage, during intermission, and at the end of the show. It was ritual.

One evening during the run, I was invited to a party by Dr. Maurice Saklad, a prominent New York dentist I had met through Leo Durocher. The party was in honor of a physician who had just returned from Canada. Since I never drank before a performance, I was having a ginger ale and my usual cigarette.

Dr. Saklad introduced the guest of honor and suggested to him, "Tell Ricardo about that interesting conference you attended in Canada."

"Oh no, I see he's enjoying his cigarette. I don't want to spoil it for him."

"No, I'm interested," I said. "It won't bother me. I know smoking is bad for your health, but I enjoy it. Maybe I'll get run over by a truck or hit by a stray bullet. So what if I live five or six years less by smoking? I enjoy it."

"All right, then, I'll tell you," said the physician. He explained that the conference had been attended by twelve of the leading lung and respiratory experts. They studied overwhelming evidence that smoking caused cancer and also constricted the blood vessels, making the heart labor to pump. One study pointed out the prevalence of respiratory cancer among Catholic priests who smoked and not among Catholic nuns, who didn't smoke.

"Very interesting," I agreed. "But it won't happen to me."

The physician continued his report, adding that a dozen psychiatrists had also been asked to attend the conference. They were asked for help in how to convince patients to give up smoking, an extremely difficult thing for smokers to do.

One psychiatrist supplied the motivation for smokers: the comfort of the customary. He explained that every human being suffers trauma in being born; he is spanked and enters the world crying. His first great satisfaction is to go to the mother's breast and enjoy the warmth and love and nourishment. It is a beautiful experience for the infant.

When the child is in the cradle and starts to cry, the psychiatrist added, eventually the thumb finds its way to the mouth. This duplicates the pleasurable, calming experience at the mother's breast. He finds comfort in the customary.

After the child has grown older, he asks his mother, "Tell me the story of Snow White and the Seven Dwarfs." She protests that she has repeated the story seventeen times, but he still wants the story. He knows that it will be entertaining, it will have no surprises, and it will end happily.

The child becomes a man, and he goes to a friend's house for dinner. After the meal he returns to the living room and takes the same chair he sat in before dinner. When he goes to the theater, he enters through the right or the left door, according to his custom, and sits in the same part of the theater. The psychiatrist offered other examples of how people find comfort in what is customary to them.

The conversation went on to other subjects, but I kept thinking about what the physician had said. Later that night I glanced at the cigarette I was smoking. I thought, "Do I need this to help me feel secure? Am I that weak that I need this crutch to make me feel like a man?"

"I don't need this," I said. I rubbed out the cigarette and I never smoked again.

I wish I could say that the argument had appealed to my logic. It didn't. My *pride* was affected, and that reason was strong enough so I never missed smoking again.

I never issued edicts to my children about smoking. When one of my sons was in the university, I came home and found his room filled with smoke. He had been smoking while he did his homework, and he quickly put out the cigarette. He seemed embarrassed.

"If you are embarrassed because you think you were disrespectful, that's all right," I told him. "But if you are embarrassed because you think you did something wrong, I will tell you that it is not immoral or illegal to smoke. I have *suggested* that you don't smoke only because of your health and well-being, not because it is immoral or illegal. I can't tell you *not* to smoke, because I smoked myself when I was your age. It's just not a very bright idea."

I don't know if the message got across, but I managed to convey it in another way. We often played tennis together. I was the more advanced player, but because he was more athletic, he could return virtually all the balls I hit to him. One day I systematically hit to his left, then his right, left and right, over and over again. By the end of the set, he was huffing and puffing and I was not even breathing hard—not only because I wasn't running hard, but because I had quit smoking years before. I think my son realized that if he had so little wind at such an early age, then smoking was not the best thing in the world for him. I believe he smokes much less or hardly at all now.

My father often said, "Use and abuse—that is the difference between enjoying something and letting it become a sin."

From the time that I was very young, I remember there was always a bottle of wine on the table. Each child had a glass of water, and my father poured a little wine into it. Thus we children felt like a part of the family; we weren't being deprived of something special. As we grew older, we were given a little sip of the wine, then half a glass. My father believed that wine was a complement to dinner; it rinsed the mouth and heightened the taste of the food. It was not a drink for its own sake. It was part of the pleasure of eating.

So drinking became a natural and pleasurable part of my life. When I became twenty-one, there was not great change in my habits because I could then drink legally.

To me it is a mistake to ask a young person to refrain from alcohol and then tell him at the age of twenty-one, "*Now* you can drink all you want." It's almost a license to get drunk.

I followed my father's pattern when my children were growing up. Each of them had a little wine at the table if they desired it, and I believe they all learned how to handle drinking. One of my sons had a harder lesson, however.

The whole family went to Malibu for a weekend at the beach house of Maggie and Jean Louis. One evening after dinner, my son took two of the Louis's pug dogs for a walk on the beach after dinner. He climbed over rocks to the next beach and met a friend. The friend was bored and looking for adventure. "Let's get a bottle of wine," he suggested.

Since both boys were fifteen, they couldn't purchase wine. They walked across Pacific Coast Highway to the liquor store and convinced a customer to buy them a couple of bottles of cheap wine. The two boys sat on the beach drinking the wine and feeling very grown-up—and then very sick.

Somehow my son managed to crawl over the rocks and reach our house. I was awakened by a pounding at the bedroom door. I looked out and saw a strange, wet creature I couldn't identify. Was it a thief, a maniac, a derelict washed up from the ocean? As I looked closer, I saw who it was.

He was violently ill. I put him under the shower, clothes and all, got him undressed and into pajamas, and put him to bed. There was no need for lectures, then or in the morning. The monumental hangover told him better than I could the lesson of Use and Abuse.

Father O'Mara talked to us in the chapel at Sunday noon about the Examination of Conscience:

"You exercise your body in order to keep physically fit. The Examination of Conscience is a spiritual exercise that can rejuvenate your soul and keep you conscious of the role that Christ must play in your life.

Try it. Take time at noon and before you go to sleep to examine your actions and beliefs. Two acts of perfect contrition every day can have a spiritual effect, bringing you closer to God."

I resolved to do it. I had thought of doing it before: "Isn't that a lovely idea? But so impractical. How can I stop my life twice every day to make an assessment?" I can do it. Instead of listening to the big-band music on the radio, I could spend five minutes on the freeway to examine my thoughts and actions.

It is like looking at the rushes at the studio. I study the previous day's work, and I ponder, "I don't like that. How can I correct it?" or, "That is good; I should continue doing it."

I could see many areas for improvement.

I always considered myself well informed, allowing for my limited intellect. But I realize that I am guilty of not putting more into that intellect. The mind is just like the body: it needs to be exercised. How lazy I have been not to study more, not to feed more information into that computer that is the mind. Only by absorbing information can it grow in perception.

I realize that I could be a better husband to Georgiana. At times I can become petty; I still have the machismo syndrome that is common to the Latin temperament. Atavism is hard to eradicate, but I keep trying.

As an actor I find myself falling into the temptation of resenting the success of my fellow performers and hoping for their failure. Jealousy comes easily in my profession, which is enormously competitive. That is wrong. I should be joyful when other actors succeed, not resentful.

Most of all, I should have more understanding of those who disagree with me. It is easy to love that which is lovable. How much more difficult to love those whose ideas are prickly, those who seem different and foreign. Certainly I, of all people, should have learned that lesson.

Vietnam, 1971. I had gone to that tortured land for two reasons. One was to see my son Mark, who was serving in the U. S. Army. The other was to go on a "handshake tour," visiting and talking with soldiers and sailors at military installations, hospitals, and outposts. Most of my military experience came from watching John Wayne movies, and I expected the army to be filled with lusty, brawling characters. It wasn't. I found the army men to be like Americans in any walk of life—some fun-loving, some serious, some talkative, some quiet. I found no one to fit my stereotype of the army man—until I arrived at Fire Station 37.

I stepped out of the helicopter at the desolate outpost and was greeted by Sergeant Stone. At last I had found the quintessential sergeant—red-faced, thick-necked, with beer belly and blustery manner. As I leaned over to avoid the propeller blades, I could see the disdain in his face. I could almost hear him thinking, "What the hell is this Hollywood actor doing out here?"

He gave me a handshake, and suddenly I felt the blood draining from my hand. "Hello, I'm Sergeant Stone," he said, tightening the vise.

"I'm Ricardo Montalban; nice to meet you," I said, giving him back as much pressure as I could manage.

"I suppose you want to see the men," he grunted.

"That's what I'm here for."

"Follow me."

He marched off through the ankle-deep mud, and I followed behind. We met a few of the soldiers, and Sergeant Stone muttered, "Here's the movie star they promised you." It was a difficult position for me to be in, because I couldn't entertain them. The idea of the tours was simply to bring a little diversion into the dreary lives of the young men away from home. Fortunately, there had been advance publicity and they knew I was coming. They had even been shown some of my pictures. So I broke the ice by asking where they were from, and soon they were asking questions about what was going on in the States. Then they brought out the cameras and I posed with them. It was an extremely heartwarming and rewarding experience for me, and the soldiers seemed to be having a good time.

Sergeant Stone watched all this as he took me from one group to another. His attitude seemed to change slowly. He saw the enjoyment on the men's faces, and perhaps he concluded that this wasn't a Hollywood show-off after all.

It was time for me to leave, and Sergeant Stone walked me back to the helicopter. A corporal took a last photograph, and the sergeant motioned to him. "Hey, Murphy, I want ya to take my picture," he called. He turned to me and said, "Okay?"

"Why, certainly, Sergeant, it would be a pleasure," I said, and I put an arm around his shoulder, as I had done with the other men.

As the corporal was focusing the camera, Sergeant Stone said to me, "This is for my wife. Personally, I don't give a shit."

Just as I had my own notion of what army men would be like, so Sergeant Stone had his own prestamped idea about film actors. That's what I hate: stamps.

Hollywood has always been guilty of applying stamps. This actor is a Latin lover. That actress is a sexpot. Always stamps.

It happens in our everyday life. These people are lazy and shiftless. Those people are crooks and thieves. The stamps become stereotypes and fester into prejudice.

I knew what it was like to be prejudged as a son of Spaniards in Mexico, later as a Mexican in the United States. Could it be possible that I could succumb to prejudicial thinking? I couldn't imagine it. And yet . . .

It's amazing how anyone can fall prey to prejudice merely

by constant exposure. I think you find less of it in the entertainment business, where most of us realize what nonsense it is to judge a person by his skin color or his family's origin. But you do come in contact with people who perpetuate stereotypes, either out of ignorance or malice. Listen to them enough and your computer brain starts to imprint such nonsense as valid information.

"If you're boxing a black man, hit him in the stomach or the kidneys, not the head. You'll never knock him out on the head because it's too hard."

Nonsense. And yet if you hear it often enough, you may start believing it. And maybe I did. As a boy, the only blacks I saw were baseball players from Vera Cruz, and they were heroes. Later at MGM, I worked with black actors whom I admired enormously.

It was in *Jamaica* that I became totally color-blind.

I was the only white man in the cast. Any remnants of prejudice that I might have had were wiped out by that experience. Not only did I find Lena Horne to be a supreme artist and warm human being; the rest of the cast were gentle, humorous, immaculate, and full of the joy of life.

There was one exception. He used to come to my dressing room while I was being made up, and he delighted in dishing out the gossip of the company. He kept pouring out the malicious stuff, and I kept saying, "Yes . . . yes," even when I detested what he was saying.

Finally one day I said impulsively, "Look, I don't want to hear all that gossip anymore. I'm up to my ears in it. So please stop."

I suddenly realized I had been treating him differently because he was black. No race has a monopoly on goodness or badness; we're all a mixture of both. I should have evaluated him as a human being, and ultimately I did. I believe that was the moment when I truly became blind to color.

Jamaica was considered daring in its time because I, a white man, played a romance with Lena Horne. During the run, I received many letters that read like this:

> Dear Judas,
> How could you possibly kiss a member of the black race on the stage and then go home to your wife and your children? I used to enjoy your movies but I won't anymore.
>
> Your ex-fan

There is nothing you can do about such hate mail, nothing you can reply. I could only wish that the writer could get to know those people in *Jamaica*. The hate would have disappeared. You can love only that which you know. If people of other backgrounds would *really* get to know those of other colors, religions, and national origins, then the word *prejudice* would not exist in our vocabularies.

I had always been aware of the prejudice that existed against Mexican Americans. When I was in high school in Los Angeles, I remembered that some of my fellow students tried to hide the *burritos* and *tacos* that their mothers had packed in their lunches. To eat such things was to be "different"; it was safer to consume the sterile sandwiches consisting of two slices of white bread and a slab of meat.

Perhaps I was naïve to believe that prejudice could not touch me as an actor in Hollywood. I had an abrupt awakening one day in the early 1960s when a producer called me to his office to discuss a proposed television series.

"Ricardo, I think I've found a way to solve your problem," said the producer.

That gave me pause. I wasn't aware that I had a problem, outside of the one that all actors face in finding jobs.

"I got this idea for a series," he continued. "You will play a cop from the other side of the border who will work in concert with a cop from *this* side of the border. He'll be blond, blue-eyed, and clean-cut."

"Hmmm," I thought, "what does that make me—dirty-cut?"

Nothing ever came of the producer's idea, but the conversation had a profound effect on me. It made me aware of the prejudice that existed not only in the community, but in the world of television and motion pictures.

In 1970 I met with a group of Mexican Americans headed by two bright young men, Robert Apodaca and Gil Avila. Some of them were actors or had some part in the entertainment business. Others were lawyers or businessmen. All were concerned.

"Ricardo, you know these are very tense times in the Mexican-American community," said Avila. "Our people are seeking their identity, and that's why they're adopting the name Chicano."

"We feel we could do something to ease the tension," said Apodaca, "and also to help right certain wrongs. Specifically, we're talking about the entertainment industry, where the image of our people has been so damaging, so demeaning."

"I agree," I replied. "What can I do to help?"

"We have no entrée to the studios and the networks, no way to talk to writers, producers, and directors," Avila said. "We need a key to open those doors. You could be the key."

I thought about it. I had never been a political activist. And yet I felt strongly that the image of Mexico and Mexicans had been damaged for a great many years. Coming from Mexico, I felt that my native country had been betrayed by Hollywood. I realized that the film makers had not purposely aimed to be damaging; they were simply adding color to their movies. A bank teller doing his daily job is not colorful. A lawyer is not colorful, nor a scientist. But a man sleeping under a cactus tree or a bandit with a big mustache and a big hat and bandoleers across his chest—they are colorful. At least that is what I like to believe: that Hollywood had perpetuated those images not out of malice, but out of ignorance about what harm it was doing by presenting such caricatures.

I felt compelled to say, "Let's go!" But first I discussed the matter with several people whose opinions I respected, including actors.

"Don't do it, Ricardo," a fellow actor told me. "This can be counterproductive. Once you take a stand, you are going to be respected by the people who agree with your stand, and you are going to be despised by those who don't agree. It's tough enough to be an actor and try to get the majority of people to like your work. Once you take a stand, you really put your reputation on the line. If more people despise what you are doing than agree with you, then it can be extremely harmful."

"If there is no risk involved, there is no virtue in it," I replied. "I believe in it strongly, and I'm willing to sacrifice whatever it takes to help these people open a few doors."

So I agreed to join the cause. But I had to do it my way. I am not a militant. I believe that in a war against injustice you have to employ all kinds of weapons. You desperately need a militant group that brings awareness to the community, voices that are loud and clear. You also need a diplomatic corps that can follow through, and formulate and negotiate the remedies that must be made. I felt I could contribute in a small way by establishing a dialogue with film makers and try to ease the situation that I knew well. I don't know anything about the barrio. I'm not a product of barrio; I come from Torreón, Mexico. I don't know anything about the farm workers, for all my sympathy, understanding, and admiration that I have for Cesar Chavez. But I do know the motion picture industry, and in that area, I thought I could contribute something. I agreed to become the first president.

The name for the new organization: Nosotros.

I had done a film in Mexico titled *Nosotros,* and it was the title of a popular song. It means "we." Therefore it signified We of Spanish-speaking Origin. Not only Mexican, but South American and Spanish, too.

Consider the Mexican-American children of Los Angeles, who *are* Americans. They sit in front of the television set and they have nothing to identify with—except bandits and sleepy peons. A Mexican-American mother told us of overhearing a conversation between her two young children.

"I'll bet you don't even know what a Mexican is," said the seven-year-old.

"Sure I do," said the five-year-old.

"Okay, what is a Mexican?"

"Frito Bandito." The boy's only connection with his own heritage was a cartoon caricature of a six-shooter bandit in a corn chip commercial.

It's tragic. The boy did not realize what his people had achieved. For instance . . .

In World War II, two National Guard regiments composed almost entirely of Mexican Americans set records for valor in Bataan and on Corregidor. Their example prompted heavy enlistments, and 375,000 Mexican Americans served during World War II and the Korean War. Mexican Americans comprised 10 per cent of the population of Los Angeles County during that time; casualty lists in the local papers included 20 per cent with Hispanic names. Nineteen Congressional Medal of Honor winners had Hispanic names. The two Congressional Medal of Honor winners from Los Angeles County were Eugene Obregon of East Los Angeles and David Gonzalez of Pacoima. Unfortunately, these were not the kinds of Mexican-American heroes that a five-year-old could identify with.

We carried our Nosotros message to film makers, particularly writers because they provide the material. We implored them to help give hope to Mexican-American children so they could point with pride at something that is honorable and good, so they could say, "We could be that someday; we could do it, too."

Doors were opened to us. Wherever we asked for appointments to present our views, it was arranged. When the Writers Guild of America was having a meeting about a strike vote, I was allowed five minutes to tell about the people of the barrio, who love their country but wonder if they love it more than it loves them. They live in cities that bear names like Los Angeles, San Francisco, Sacramento, San Diego, Salinas, San Jose, yet they feel like strangers in their own land. That was why they now called themselves Chicanos. They are not Mexicans; many of them don't even speak Spanish. They are Americans. But wait a minute—*are* they Americans? Not according to the communication media.

One of the aims of Nosotros was to promote opportunities for our people to play roles that called for actors of Spanish-speaking origin—or any roles they were capable of playing. But we realized we had to be ready when those opportunities came, and so we aimed to establish an acting workshop. Actors could then learn diction, perform scenes, do improvisations, so they would be prepared for challenges of acting jobs.

That took money. One of our members was Tony DeMarco, who had staged Mexican extravaganzas for Disneyland and other places. He suggested, "Why don't we rent the Hollywood Bowl and put on a show to raise funds?"

The Hollywood Bowl! We were staggered by the prospect of filling the place. But Tony convinced us we could do it. I sent letters to a list of entertainers, asking if they would join the show to benefit Nosotros. The first reply came from Frank Sinatra: "Of course I'll be there." Dionne Warwicke, who was my next-door neighbor at the time, also agreed to perform. With Sinatra and Warwicke we had a show, and many other entertainers joined the cast, including the Mexican star Antonio Aguilar.

The benefit was a real success, and it allowed us to establish the actors' workshop. Now we had to educate casting offices and producers to hire actors of Spanish-speaking origin. We asked no favors. We simply asked that such people be *considered* for acting opportunities.

What often happened was that an agent might suggest a client named Garcia to a casting director. The reply: "No, we don't have any parts for Mexicans in this picture."

"But he doesn't have an accent," the agent protested.

"I don't care. I don't want to waste my time."

We were asking employers not to reject a prospect because of his name. Give him the dignity of being able to present his talent. Then if you don't think he's suitable, hire someone else. But at least give him a chance.

Enrique Delgado was a highly competent New York actor, a Puerto Rican without an accent. He auditioned for many stage productions, including Shakespeare and other classics, and he was successful, both on and off Broadway. He was encouraged to try his luck in Hollywood. He couldn't get inside the studio door. He changed his name to Henry Darrow and started getting roles, including one of the leads in the "High Chaparral" television series.

Many other actors got nowhere until they anglicized their names. We thought that was unfair.

I think that Nosotros accomplished some good. We weren't the only ones; there were other organizations that created more noise. They were hard-working and militant, and they made no nonsense about their demands. I like to believe that advances were achieved by a combination of their militancy and our own gentle persuasion. Together we managed to get rid of Frito Bandito.

There had been many protests about the television stereotype. I personally called the president of Frito-Lay and told him, "I'm telephoning you because I'd like to think that I'm the voice of reason. This Frito Bandito is like the straw that breaks the camel's back."

"Why?" he replied. "I think it's a very cute little fellow."

"Precisely because he's cute he is very insidious. Why didn't you make him the Frito Amigo, giving the chips away, sharing them with everyone because he loves them so? No. You make him a *bandit*, stealing the chips. Because that's the only way to think of a Mexican—as a bandit."

"You know, I never thought of it that way."

I don't know what influence I had, but Frito Bandito did disappear from television. So has the Mexican bandit. But unfortunately I don't see many Mexican-American actors on television, either. This is unfortunate, especially in Los Angeles, where Chicanos are the largest minority by far. They are almost invisible on television.

I believe that Nosotros accomplished some good, though not necessarily for Ricardo Montalban. I was the victim of a backlash which I felt was an injustice.

At an early meeting I remarked, "Of course there must be antagonists in any drama. If you're doing a Western that takes place on the border and you need a Mexican bandit for a heavy, all right. There are Mexican bandits, Chinese bandits, American bandits—no nation has a monopoly.

"If you have a Mexican bandit, don't make him a caricature. Make him a human being. Give him a heartbeat, find out what kind of a person he is.

"If Eli Wallach can play a Mexican bandit better than I can, I would be enough of a professional to insist that he play the role. All we ask is that we are allowed to compete with Eli Wallach, not only for the part of the Mexican bandit but for any part we are capable of performing."

A trade paper reporter who attended the meeting quoted me as saying, "We are tired of Anglos playing us."

If I had been another actor reading that, I would have thought Montalban to be a bigoted and dumb individual. If only Mexicans should play Mexican roles, then should only Danes play Hamlet? How much Mexican blood was required to play Mexican roles? And so forth. It was ridiculous. An actor should have no frontiers, no barriers. Only his talent should matter.

A week later I saw the reporter when I was working at Universal. I told him, "Look, your paper has done a terrible disservice, and I would like a clarification of what I said." I outlined what I had really said, and I added, "Doesn't it stand to reason that if good Greek and Italian actors can successfully play Mexicans, then good Mexican actors could conceivably play Greeks and Italians? Doesn't that make sense?"

The "clarification" appeared in the paper the following day: "We ran into Ricardo Montalban, president of Nosotros, on a set at Universal and he said, 'Why should Greeks and Italians play Mexicans?'"

I'm sure that all Greek and Italian actors have hated me ever since. And no doubt producers and directors said, "What is this guy bellyaching about? He's made a good living in this country. Why does he stir up trouble?"

I suffered because of the misquotations. For four years I never made a movie. Television roles became scarce, and I was offered only roles that were basically Mexican, whereas I had played a wide variety before. Producers didn't hire me, and they were right—*if* I had actually said what I had been quoted as saying.

The stage offered me a chance to earn a living, and so I survived. Then the Chrysler Corporation chose me as spokesman on television for the Cordoba, and that exposure helped turn things around. I started to work again in Hollywood.

Will Rogers used to say, "All I know is what I read in the newspapers." If that was true, then I fear he harbored a lot of misinformation. I discovered it was impossible to make my point clear and have it reported correctly.

I have no regrets. You choose a route, you go with it, and you pay the consequences. It was perhaps inevitable that I would be misjudged, just as I was misjudged as a boy because I spoke the Castilian of my parents. I was born in Mexico, and I loved my country with my very being, but that did not mean I could not love Spain, which had given me my parents. And so it is now. When I love the United States, does that mean that

I must love Mexico less? I don't think so. We develop many loves during our journey through life—love of parents, of brothers and sisters, of teachers and sweethearts. We don't need to sacrifice one for another.

So much to think about. As the hours at Manresa began reaching to the end, I found my mind was filled with reflections on my life and faith.

It will take time to absorb it all. Only by being fed information can you learn, but the digestion doesn't come all at once. Sometimes you get indigestion. That happens when the enzymes are not functioning properly. So you take an antacid tablet to restore the balance, and the information becomes part of your system.

That's not enough. It's one thing to be exposed to an idea, another to put it into practice.

The retreat weekend made me realize how lazy I have been. I have known the spiritual exercises, but too often I have failed to practice them.

Father O'Mara had continued with the analogy of building a house—first finding firm ground, then laying a sturdy foundation, building the structure according to a sound plan, then decorating it with taste and artistry.

That's not enough. Then you must keep the house from falling into disrepair. You must replace lost shingles, clean clouded windows, wipe off fingerprints on the doors. The beauty of the house could be destroyed without the upkeep.

There should be no room in life for pettiness. I should be rejoicing in the good fortune of others and lamenting their setbacks. I believe with St. Francis of Assisi that in giving we receive.

When I see something impressive on television, I

call, "Georgie, come and see this." I want to share it with her. Or I say, "This plum is delicious; have a taste." Seeing her enjoy it gives me more joy than the taste I took myself.

I remember as a boy in Mexico I was taught to give my seat to a woman in a streetcar or bus if all the other seats were occupied. She would say *"Gracias,"* and that compensated for having to stand in the aisle. I had relinquished my seat out of good manners, but I was doubly rewarded by her thanks.

How can I translate this into my work? It is easy to do in front of a camera. I have always felt that my occupation should be "reactor," not actor. The more I give to the other actor, the more I receive.

The important thing is to make a scene work, to be truthful, to come to life. I'm very pragmatic about that.

There are two extremes in playing a scene. You can underplay for the sake of underplaying; then the scene becomes lame, it has no vitality. Or you can try to "steal" the scene, in which case you have nothing. You have achieved nothing by trying to aggrandize yourself. In the final analysis, you are a ham—and ham eventually becomes rancid.

In real life, I let my emotions carry me away; that is a Latin trait that I cannot always control. In my professional life, I try to channel those emotions into something that gives the character life. All my faults are usable, but they must be distilled. When that distillation process is completed, then I must "react" with my fellow player, giving him or her the best possible support.

Sometimes other actors question me about my faith. It usually happens after we have had a drink or two. Then the friend is emboldened to inquire, "Why are you a Catholic, Ricardo?"

I don't mind that. I welcome the opportunity to articulate, if only to myself, why I believe as I do. My friend is asking partly out of curiosity, partly out of concern for me. He wants to make sure that I am not deluding myself with empty rituals. And perhaps he is inquiring because of his own misplaced faith.

The only time I don't enjoy such probing is when the questioner engages in ridicule: "Come on, Ricardo, you don't really believe all that mumbo jumbo, do you? This is the twentieth century!"

It's not possible to convince such a scoffer of how much value my faith adds to my life, in my day-to-day living and in times of great sorrow.

"Ricardo, you must go to Torreón."

The face of my brother Carlos was grim, his words were measured. I realized the gravity of the matter. Why else would he come backstage before a performance of *Jamaica?*

"Father is not well," Carlos continued. "It is absolutely impossible for me to leave New York. You know I would go if there were any way. I have spoken to Mr. Merrick. He says it is all right for you to leave the show. I will join you in a couple of days. I think you should be with Mother and Carmen."

I made my entrance onstage in a daze, and I will never know how I got through the performance. When I returned to the dressing room at intermission, Georgiana had arrived. Then I knew.

"Father is dead, isn't he?" I asked Carlos.

"Yes," my brother replied.

The journey to Torreón was arduous. After long flights, I arrived at Juárez, rented a car and drove to Monterrey, then west to Torreón. I drove through the night, without sleep. The shock did not lessen. My father's death was the first in our immediate family, the first death that had struck me deeply. My emotions were in a turmoil.

I drove directly to my sister's house. Mother was there, and she was without tears. She had cried all she could cry. "Come and see your father," she said.

I was appalled. The undertaker had used cosmetics to try for a pleasant expression on my father's face, and it seemed grotesque. A lifeless face on a man who possessed so much life. It gave me too much pain to look at his face, and my eyes drifted to his hands. They were placed across his chest with a rosary in their grasp. They were pale, but the hands had not changed. Those were the hands I had known and loved, which had chastised me with much-deserved punishment, but always out of love. Now that I had children of my own, I understood how hard it is for a father to administer spankings. I remembered the sting I had received from my own father's hands, but I realized the intent was good. How much I loved those hands!

On the morning of the funeral, it rained. Torreón had endured a seven-year drought, but now it rained. The trip to the cemetery seemed even more mournful because of the weather. When the coffin was lowered into the ground and the first shovelful of mud was thrown on it, I was overwhelmed with grief. I wanted to jump into that grave and get my father out.

Mother never fully recovered from my father's death.

The suddenness of his passing was too great a shock after fifty-three years of total devotion. Her mind started to wander. She would sit in a chair saying her Rosary, then look up and say, "Jenaro, when you go to play dominoes, would you please stop at the baker on the way back? You know the cookies I like, the ones with the coconut. I would like a dozen. And if you should think of it, perhaps a half dozen of the chocolate. Now go along and have a good time." And she returned to her Rosary.

My sister's devotion to her was extraordinary. Carmen would not even consider putting Mother in a home for the aged. Carmen and her husband and their children gave Mother the care and attention she needed, and she remained in their home until the end.

Once more I was summoned to Torreón. Mother was failing fast, Carmen had told me. We all converged—Carlos from New York, Pedro from Mexico City, I from Los Angeles. When I visited Mother in her bedroom, her eyes were staring forward at some focal point in the distance. The breath came heavily from her chest. "Look at this," said Carmen, turning down the blanket. Mother's hands were empty, but the fingers were moving as if she were counting her Rosary.

All of us stayed with her through the afternoon, went out for dinner, and returned for the evening vigil. I lingered on when the others went to bed. "I wonder if she knows we're here," I thought, and I decided to try an experiment. I placed myself within her line of vision and backed up until I noticed that the eyes focused.

"Mama, this is your Chato," I said. That was what she called me as I was growing up, because in my early years I had a pug nose. "I love you so much, Mama, all of us do."

I poured out my heart, not knowing whether she heard or not. Then suddenly her breathing came a little faster, her eyebrows raised, and a tiny tear flowed from each eye. She knew.

I went to bed at four, and after a few hours' sleep, I was awakened with the news that Mother had died. We buried her next to Father.

My mother's death was easier for me to take, since it was not sudden, like my father's. Yes, the loss was sad, but I could also rejoice that my parents were now united with the Creator. I believe that, I know that from the depths of my soul. The mortal aspect is sad; the spiritual aspect can be absolutely uplifting.

When I was a boy, death frightened me. It doesn't anymore. I would not want a painful or a horrible death. But if I live by what I believe, then I not only have to accept death, but welcome it as the crowning glory of life—the goal of life. I believe in the hereafter, I believe in God and being reunited with Him. My whole being tells me that something in me wants to be reunited with the Creator. That's how I look at it, and that's why death no longer scares me.

Why fear death? It will happen. I've found there is no moment as awful as the moment you fearfully anticipate. I used to fret, "Damn, I have to go to the dentist and have a tooth pulled." The extraction was not as bad as my imagination built it up to be.

Again, my lesson from Japan: Savor each moment. Enjoy what you are doing *now*. Enjoy being in the hurly-burly of life, but also enjoy being with yourself. Listen to the high whine of a jet airplane, the shouts of children at play, the buzzing of insects. Listen to the silence, to your own soul.

It's imperative to grasp the moment, so you can maintain some control over your destiny. I believe you have *some* control over what happens to you, but we're really the children of chance in this world. Most of the important happenings of our lives are dictated by circumstance. That's why it is absolutely useless to look back and lament, "I wish I had done this, or that."

To me the miracle of life is to be born. What happens thereafter is not terribly important. But it is important to be born so that you can later go on to the spiritual life; unless you have existed as a human being, that eternal life cannot exist for you.

Death is being reborn. It is a sad thing for those you leave behind, those who miss you; it is a terrible tragedy to them. But since time is only relative in the corporal life and since there is no time in the spiritual life, your existence on earth is less important than what happens thereafter. What matters is the rebirth into communion with your Creator.

That doesn't mean that life on earth is unimportant. Of course it has meaning and value, and it is essential to live life to the fullest. Very few in this world have been able to get the *best* out of life. There are too many distractions, too many obligations that deter us, and often we are lazy. You never quite achieve the potential for which you were created. Nevertheless, if your intent is to do the best you can, to live fully, to be selfless and loving, then your existence on this planet is not wasted.

At one-thirty Sunday afternoon, the chapel bell— followed by the more urgent buzzer—summoned the retreatants to the last conference. David was late, of course. I had grown accustomed to seeing him limp painfully through the chapel door with a genial shrug to excuse his tardiness.

I had also grown accustomed to the refreshing cool of the chapel, with a verdant vista through the three arched windows of oaks, elms, and ferns. This was the eleventh time we had been called to the chapel during the weekend, and I had grown to love it as I did my boyhood church in Mexico.

"Gentlemen, you are nearing the end of the retreat," said Father O'Gara. "But this is not the end; it is the beginning. Like graduation from college, it is a commencement. You are commencing a new life."

He urged us to apply to our daily lives the lessons we had learned during the weekend. Especially with our wives. "The definition of a successful marriage," he said, "is self-sacrifice."

How true. If you are too involved with your own person, then you lose consideration for your partner. Only by submerging your self can you achieve a true partnership. The years have brought Georgiana and me so close that we are practically fused in our beings. So much so that I cannot conceive of life without her.

I'm certain that the long separations that we have had to endure have been healthy for our relationship. The long weeks and months that I spent on the road in plays and making films abroad have been almost like a retreat. I was able to think about Georgiana and our life together and to cherish the good things. When you are too close to a painting, you can see the brushstrokes and the flaws in the artist's technique. But when you step back a few paces, you can see the totality of the artist's concept. Separations can be dangerous for some couples, but in our case we found ourselves renewed in love and appreciation of each other. And besides, who ever said that any experience in life must be perfect? There is always a price to pay.

The retreat was over.

We came out of the chapel as exuberant as schoolboys at the end of a semester. Suddenly the stored-up words came pouring out as we walked across the veranda to the dining room for coffee and farewells. The priests, who had sometimes seemed stern and sober during the retreat, now turned absolutely jovial. They told Irish stories and reminisced about their lives in the Church.

Alas, there was little time for the retreatants to find out more about each other. All of us had our own lives to return to, and soon the freeways would be crowded with other Sunday travelers on their way home. It would be best for us to get an early start.

During the brief postlude to the retreat, I did uncover the story of David. One of the priests mentioned that he had been chaplain at a Catholic high school in Los Angeles.

"Then you must know the principal," David said haltingly. "He saved my life." David told his story:

He had been perfectly normal physically until one day when he had gone for a noon ride in another student's brand-new sports car. The other boy sped the car down a city street and lost control. The driver was thrown to the street during the spin and was unhurt. David remained inside as the car smashed against a telephone pole and was demolished. Because he was still under school supervision, the principal was able to give doctors permission to operate. David's parents could not be reached, and the minutes saved meant the difference between life and death.

David told us that he was in a coma for six months. Surgeons meanwhile operated again and again to restore his splintered arms and legs. When David regained consciousness, he not only discovered he had a broken body; brain damage had severely hindered his speech and motor control. Long months followed as he struggled to learn how to use his body and mind again.

Miraculously, he was able to complete high school and even go on to college. But his capacities were limited, he admitted, and after three years the college told him he had gone as far as he was able.

"But I haven't given up," he declared. "I'm going to junior college now, and I know I can go on and get a degree. You know something? The human brain has the capacity to restore damage that has been done. Doctors have told me that. My brain is getting better all the time. I can tell the difference."

I had to leave. Tears were forming in my eyes, and I feared they would flow down my cheeks if I stayed any longer. I said good-bye to the courageous young man, whose smiling, open face I shall always remember. If ever I should start feeling despondent and sorry for myself, I need only remember the indomitable David of the Manresa retreat.

And so I started for home, retracing the route along the Foothill Freeway to Freeway 605, then to the San

Bernardino Freeway. I felt a serenity that I hadn't known in years. Yet the feeling wasn't passive. Far from it. My mind was filled with fresh insights about God and how I could best serve Him. Resolutions poured forth.

Father O'Gara had cited the analogy of the two seas in the Holy Land. One is Galilee, which is big enough to be called a sea, even though it has an outlet. Because it gives off its water, Galilee is fresh and clean, sweet to the taste and hospitable to fish. Then there is the Dead Sea, which does not have an outlet. All the water remains there, and it becomes brackish and foul-tasting; fish cannot live, and plants on the banks wither and die.

The comparison can be made to our own living. If we are free and open and giving, our lives will be full and fruitful. But if we want to keep everything to ourselves, we will be consumed by our avarice.

Those thoughts, and a thousand others, flowed through my mind as I motored westward toward the waning sun.